Intuition
in an
Instant

ABOUT THE AUTHOR

Kathryn Klvana has been drawn to the metaphysical since she was a young girl. A decade ago, she started on a spiritual journey and discovered dowsing as a means of self-discovery and growth. Excited by the ease and practicality of dowsing and its ability to open intuitive pathways, she completely immersed herself in studying it and teaching what she learned to others. Kathryn teaches dowsing in the Washington, DC, area, and has presented dowsing workshops at the American Society of Dowsers annual conventions. Kathryn grew up on Long Island and received a BA in English from the State University of New York at Stony Brook. A professional actor and voiceover artist, she lives in Kensington, Maryland.

DISCOVER YOUR
Inner Wisdom
THROUGH
Dowsing

Intuition
in an
Instant

KATHRYN KLVANA

Llewellyn Publications
Woodbury, Minnesota

First Edition
First Printing, 2011

Cover design by Ellen Lawson
Interior illustrations on pages 32, 37, 39, 41, 93, 104 © Wen Hsu, all other
    illustrations by the Llewellyn Art Department

Llewellyn is a registered trademark of Llewellyn Worldwide Ltd.

Library of Congress Cataloging-in-Publication Data
Klvana, Kathryn, 1960–
  Intuition in an instant : discover your inner wisdom through dowsing /
by Kathryn Klvana. — 1st ed.
      p.   cm.
  Includes bibliographical references.
  ISBN 978-0-7387-2330-3
1. Dowsing. 2. Intuition--Miscellanea. I. Title.
  BF1628.K65 2011
  133.3'23—dc22

                                            2011009380

Llewellyn Publications
A Division of Llewellyn Worldwide Ltd.
2143 Wooddale Drive
Woodbury, MN 55125-2989
www.llewellyn.com

Printed in the United States of America

CONTENTS

LIST OF ILLUSTRATIONS

Introduction

If a person could become psychic by wishing for it, I would have been the Uri Geller of Williston Park by the time I was twelve. I remember sitting cross-legged on the sidewalk on Remsen Street in my suburban Long Island town as my girlfriend and I stared at each other until our eyes blurred, trying to see our auras. We played games like, "I'm thinking of a number between one and twenty; what is it?" and "Guess my favorite flower." But these forays into extrasensory perception revealed me to be completely unremarkable, at least as far as psychic ability was concerned.

Over the years, I experienced enough flashes of "knowing" to consider myself intuitive in a very ordinary kind of way. I would think about someone before they called, for instance, or have an idea for a project and meet someone shortly afterward who could help me in some way. Several times, I had precognitive dreams, where the events unfolded in real life a few days later. Was it coincidence or some kind of psychic experience? Certainly it wasn't anything I had any control over, and it really wasn't anything I could use for any practical purpose. Occasionally, when something awful was to occur, I'd get a sick feeling in my stomach—literally a gut instinct—that warned me to pay attention. That, at least, was immediately useful in my life. I learned to trust that guidance and respect what it was telling me.

Various books I read over the years suggested meditation as a way to encourage intuitive ability. What was it about stilling the mind that allowed intuitive abilities to flourish? I wasn't sure, but I figured I should give it a try.

Honestly, it was a rocky start. I'm someone who has trouble emptying my mind completely and doing nothing. I set a timer and tried to quiet my mind for ten minutes. But it was tough, and frankly I didn't see any changes in my intuitive powers.

Eventually, I realized that it was easier for me to do guided visualizations—in other words, to take myself on a journey in my mind. I have a good imagination and am adept at visualizing scenes in my head. About the same time that my meditation practice was getting stronger, I read about using a pendulum to answer questions. The idea was intriguing to me. I loved how practical and useful this dowsing skill seemed. I started practicing every morning and found that I was making progress very quickly. I learned everything I could from books and attended the annual convention of the American Society of Dowsers that summer. Soon friends were asking me to dowse for them and giving my name out to others.

I do most things in life with exuberance, and dowsing is no exception. I started sharing my dowsing skill with nearly everyone in my life, and in the process raised more than a few eyebrows. I'd pull out my pendulum and teach a few of my friends how to move it with their minds. Most remained curious skeptics, but a few have taken it up as an intuitive practice on their own.

The funny thing is that there is a part of me that remains a skeptic, as I was when I started on this dowsing journey. But I am curious about how the brain works, how intuition works, and how this amazing dowsing phenomenon works. No one knows for sure, and yet the results that dowsers achieve are hard to deny.

The reason I am so excited about dowsing is that it is a way of training ourselves to connect to our inner wisdom, our intuition. That's our birthright. It's something we are all capable of, but in Western culture we are not taught how. In this book, you will learn to do exactly that by training your brain to interpret energy patterns and fields. Dowsing is an intuitive tool that will help you master your brain waves and give you a visual signal when you're in the right state of mind to access your inner wisdom. It's almost like being hooked up to a biofeedback machine, except that your pendulum or dowsing device is "recording" your results.

If you want to lead a more intuitive life, you will be amazed by how quickly you make progress using this method. You may discover you have other latent psychic abilities, like telepathy or the ability to send healing energy to others. By learning to dowse, you have chosen what I think is the easiest, most direct path to your intuitive gifts.

Intuition is a personal thing, and you'll find that your dowsing will be unique to you. How you dowse, and the topics and questions you choose to dowse, will be up to you. Everyone has a different technique because every dowser is working within the confines of his or her own mind. If a method outlined in this book works for you, use it. If it doesn't, tailor it to suit you or use a different method that does.

Will you become a professional water dowser? Probably not. Will all your answers be correct? Certainly not. We all make mistakes, and there are many variables that can interfere with our dowsing results. But learning to dowse is like opening the door to the inner workings of your mind, and to the quantum physics secrets of the universe. Start dowsing and your vision of the world will change, I promise you.

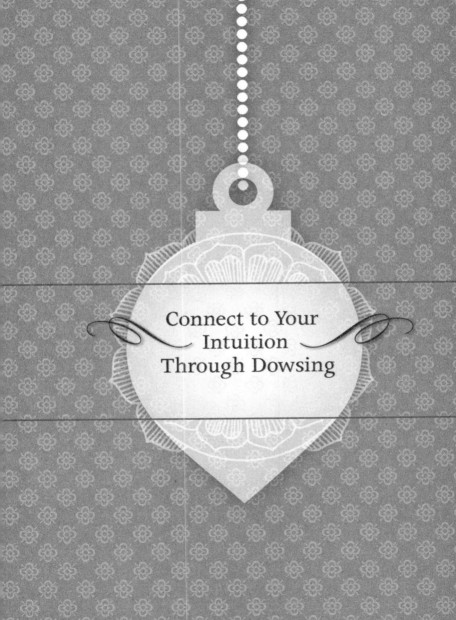

Connect to Your
Intuition
Through Dowsing

1

Basics of Dowsing

Imagine there was someone in your life you could call at any hour of the day or night to ask whatever popped into your head. No question would be too big or too small. This person could help you make tough decisions about business projects, offer insights on relationships, brainstorm with you on creative endeavors, even fine-tune your diet.

The truth is that you can have that trusted advisor with you right now, wherever and whenever you need. All you have to do is learn to tap your intuition through dowsing.

If the word *dowsing* brings to mind an image of an old-timer walking a field with a stick in his hands, you're not alone. But it's so much more than that. Dowsing is simply a word to describe an intuitive technique for getting information outside of the five senses.

When asking intuitive questions, most people prefer to use a pendulum instead of a Y-rod, the official name of the classic "forked stick." A pendulum is an object dangling from a string or chain. My life has been incredibly enriched since I picked up my first pendulum in a rock store in Woodstock, New York, several years ago. I walked in as a complete novice. I had no idea what to look for in a pendulum. I had never handled one before. But I was drawn to a beautiful, faceted one made of rose quartz. I liked the weight of it and the way light filtered through its tip, sending patterns across the palm of my hand. The saleswoman assured me that was the one I wanted. She mentioned "vibrations" and said she sensed my world was "just going to open up" that year. I nodded as if I understood what she was saying. Then I watched as she energetically cleansed the pendulum, pulling stale energy off with her hand. Right, I thought. Pretty "out there."

Here I am a few years later with a pendulum in my purse, on my bedside table, in my car, and tucked into the mortar and pestle in my kitchen. I don't go anywhere without a pendulum. It's a constant companion. And, yes, I energetically clear my crystal pendulum from time to time, just like that woman in Woodstock.

The ability to dowse is something we all carry inside us. It is a natural gift that can be accessed simply, whenever we need to engage with our intuition and gain wisdom from our higher self. But modern life is so demanding, it can be hard to cultivate intuition. We spend our days experiencing life with our five senses. We are rational, conscious, active beings. We lead linear lives. However, if we learned to call on our sixth sense, our intuition, we could delve into the hidden, unconscious part of our mind. Within this unknown, untapped part of us is the secret to dowsing. That's where we learn to connect to the energy frequencies that surround us, and to access the truth of "what is."

Some people don't need a pendulum or other dowsing tool to know these truths. They access their intuition spontaneously and naturally. Either they were born that way, or they've learned how to become sensitive to the information they are receiving. But there's help for those of us who are not born psychics. When you pick up a pendulum, you amplify the vibrations that you don't even realize you are receiving. You become more sensitive. It's like putting on a special pair of goggles that let you see something that's invisible to the naked eye. It's a tool that allows you to perceive information through your sixth sense, your "extra" sense. Pick up the pendulum and turn on your intuition. It's that easy. When you want to turn off the intuitive pipe-line, simply put your pendulum away. There is nothing overwhelming about accessing your intuitive gifts with dowsing. You are in control at all times.

There's also nothing to fear about the process. Dows-ing is not occult or supernatural. It is a practical skill that calls upon your higher self—the part of your being that communicates with the divine. If you are a spiritual person, you may find it comforting to connect to your spiritual guides or guardian angels when you pick up a pendulum. If that feels awkward to you, or if words like *the divine* and *angels* set off a strong negative reac-tion, you might find it easier to ask your higher self to connect with "the energy of the universe," or simply "pure truth and light." Use language and images that work for you.

Since ancient times, humans have used divining rods as essential survival tools. Driven by our basic need for water, dowsing has been programmed into our DNA. Some of the earliest evidence of dowsing includes two-thousand-year-old rock carvings in Peru and ancient Egyptian sculptures depicting the use of forked sticks,[1] and there are references to willow divining rods in the fifth-century B.C. writings of Herodotus, the Greek his-torian considered the father of Western history.[2] By the Middle Ages, however, dowsing and divination were looked down upon by the church. Martin Luther even condemned the use of the rod as a violation of the first commandment, "Thou shalt have no other gods before me."[3] Today, there is still some religious opposition to dowsing. Since dowsing enhances self-reliance and re-inforces the direct connection between one's own consciousness and the universal source, that is not surprising. But some Christian sects wrongly claim that dowsing is an occult act or "the work of the devil." Nothing is further from the truth. In fact, many people feel that they have become more spiritual through the use of dowsing, because it has given them a tangible way to connect to their spiritual guides.

Dowsing's usefulness in mining helped foster its acceptance, especially in Germany. A massive treatise on mining, *De Re Metallica (On Metals)*, was written in the 1500s by a German physician and scholar. It features a woodcut showing a landscape filled with mining activity, including dowsers walking with rods in their hands and miners cutting branches to fashion into divining rods. The Germans were so skilled in their mining abilities that Queen Elizabeth I brought some of them over to help locate tin, copper, and other ores in the Cornwall area.[4]

But as important as dowsing has been over the ages, the skill has largely been forgotten today. It is primarily thought of as a folksy way to find water with a forked stick, not as the eminently useful life skill that it is.

For dowsers in America today, the technique is a true gift. A survey sent to the nearly three thousand members of the American Society of Dowsers asked questions about how people use dowsing in their lives. Most use dowsing on a daily basis, and nearly all (92 percent) agree that dowsing has changed their lives for the better. Those who responded to the survey were an older, more experienced group overall. The majority had been dowsing for more than ten years, and a whopping 94 percent were over forty-five years of age. Most preferred working with a pendulum, although L-rods and deviceless dowsing also ranked high on the list. The most popular topics were dowsing for information (81 percent) and health and well-being (78 percent), while dowsing for water was only 38 percent.[5]

The potential uses of dowsing, though, are endless. You can use it as a tool for self-exploration, to better understand your subconscious motivations. You can assess the state of your health and the effectiveness of the vitamins, supplements, and medications you are taking. In business, you can pull out your pendulum to prioritize your tasks and create new opportunities for yourself. If you're looking for work, the pendulum can be valuable in determining which fields are best to pursue, when the time is right to make a move, and which job offer is best. Dowsing can also help you to understand conflicts in your relationships, both at the office and at home.

Making decisions becomes so much easier once you master dowsing. Should I take on this client? Is this food in my body's best interest? Should I drive an alternate route to work today? Do my plants need watering? Is this the car I should buy? What is the right offer to make on the house? There is no limit to the questions you can answer by dowsing with a pendulum.

However, be careful not to rely on it exclusively or excessively. Dowsing is not infallible. It is just another source of information to take into consideration when making a decision. Timing is a factor to consider as well. The answer you get one week might be very different the following week, depending on what other circumstances have changed.

Some people have told me that they are afraid to use the pendulum because they are afraid of what it will tell them. But there isn't anything more risky about dowsing than about trusting your gut instinct, or going with a hunch. This technique, after all, is a way to connect to your intuitive mind. That doesn't mean you have to follow the advice you get. I tell students that when my father was alive, I would check with him about all the important decisions I needed to make—but I didn't always follow his advice. It is wise to make a decision based on many different sources of information. Intuition is just one of them.

Used properly, dowsing can be an incredibly accurate tool to gauge the conditions that exist at that precise moment in time. The key to success with the pendulum and other dowsing tools is learning how to ask the right questions. This book will explore how to phrase questions to increase your accuracy. Learning to hold a question in your mind, and reaching out to the universe for the answer, is a technique that will help train your mind to easily fall into an intuitive brain wave pattern. Dowsing is all about "getting your mind right." Let's start off by looking at what happens inside us when we dowse, and what science can tell us about this technique for accessing our intuition.

2

How It Works: The Science Behind Dowsing

Leroy Bull doesn't have to leave his Doylestown, Pennsylvania, home when he works for clients, unless he wants to. Bull is an expert at map dowsing and possesses the focused intention that seems to be a common trait among the best professional dowsers.

Working on a map, he will narrow in on a handful of potential well sites, and then ask for photographs of those locations to be even more precise. Once he is satisfied, he will tell his clients not only the best site on the property for their well, but also how deep they'll have to drill to find water and how many gallons a minute it will draw—all without leaving the comfort of his home.

Mind-boggling as that may seem, Bull is not alone in this ability. Map dowsing is a quite common—although somewhat advanced—dowsing skill. (There's a good chance that you will be able to map-dowse once you work your way through this book.) But most people are completely dumbfounded and skeptical about this specialized ability. It's hard enough to believe that a dowser can pick up on the electromagnetic fields of a water vein beneath his or her feet when dowsing on site. But how on earth could someone dowse a well from thousands of miles away?

The answer may lie in something equally difficult to explain, the principles of quantum physics. We'll review some quantum theories later in this chapter and see how they apply to dowsing. But first, let's take a look at the most important element in dowsing: what is happening inside the dowser's mind. Holding an intention is critical to being able to receive the information. Dowsers have learned to master their own minds. They are consciously directing their thoughts and triggering brain states that are conducive to intuitive work. Let's take a look at exactly what those brain states are.

BRAIN STATE STUDY

Edith Jurka, MD, tested seven master dowsers at the annual convention of the American Society of Dowsers in 1982 using a special double electroencephalograph (EEG) device called the Mind Mirror.[1] It was developed by Dr. C. Maxwell Cade, considered the father of bio-feedback, to identify the different brain states of higher consciousness. Cade taught meditation and studied the consciousness of thousands of individuals, from yogis and psychics to those new to meditation. What he called an "awakened mind" was one in which all four brain wave states were activated in the right balance during meditation:

beta (13-30 Hz): the thinking, interpretive part of the mind;

alpha (8-13 Hz): the awake, resting state that is the bridge to the subconscious;

theta (4-8 Hz): the normal dream state that accesses the subconscious;

and *delta* (.5-4 Hz): the state of dreamless sleep, which when added to other brain states is a kind of intuitive "radar" that reaches out to pull in information.

Jurka explained that this "awakened mind" enabled enhanced access to deep insights from the subconscious and intuitive mind. In an article entitled "Brain Characteristics of Dowsers," she wrote, "A very few advanced people had such stability of the fifth state that they remained in the state all the time, while consciously going about their daily activities. The difference between being able to maintain the fifth state while meditating with eyes closed, and while interacting with the environment, is like a quantum jump. It is another jump to have arrived at the point where the fifth state is one's natural state of consciousness." Jurka was surprised to find, when she tested the dowsers, that they exhibited something close to this awakened fifth state not only while dowsing, but also in everyday consciousness. In contrast, Cade had found that his students would fall out of the alpha brain state as soon as they opened their eyes.

Curious about the brain states involved in dowsing, I decided to have myself tested on the Mind Mirror EEG. George Pierson, who runs Creative Mindflow in Silver Spring, Maryland, trains people in meditation techniques using the Mind Mirror.

Pierson explained that my normal brain pattern was close to the "awakened mind" pattern, although it contained more beta than was found in those most experienced in meditation. As soon as I closed my eyes, my beta quieted and the awakened mind pattern emerged, but with stronger than usual delta activity. When I formulated my dowsing question and held it in my mind, there was a huge surge of theta and delta, even before my pendulum started to move and I got my answer.

These lower, slower states of theta and, especially, delta are what distinguish the dowsing state.

In her book *Awakening the Mind,* Anna Wise explains:

Delta has also been connected with the concept of the collective unconscious. Whereas theta subconscious insight comes from the very depth of our innermost being and our profound inner spirituality, and is closer to the border of consciousness and more personally meaningful, delta unconscious insight can come from that which is more expansive than the personal or individual. Delta can provide access to a kind of universal psyche or mind. This collective unconscious is a kind of merging of the vast wealth of unconscious understanding and knowledge of humanity that in turn leads to a cosmological or cosmic consciousness.[2]

That is exactly what we do when we dowse: we reach out to the collective unconscious, to the universal mind, to find our answers. By believing this is possible, and practicing this connection over and over, we help trigger delta in our own minds and strengthen this state.

But the most critical brain state for dowsing is the alpha state, because it is the bridge to the deeper states.

Without it, we would not be able to remember any of the information we access.

GETTING INTO ALPHA

When we daydream, we are in alpha. It is the light, relaxed state between waking and dreaming. But to be able to access it whenever we want takes some practice, and the best way to practice getting into alpha is through the senses. Close your eyes and visualize the image of clouds moving swiftly across a March sky. Now, remember the taste of a lemon slice on your tongue, the smell of freshly cut grass, the feel of a feather on your skin, and, finally, the sound of a school bell. Practicing sense memory exercises like these (focusing on sight, taste, smell, feel, and sound) can help tone up your alpha muscles.

Another way to immediately trigger alpha is to close your eyes and raise them up slightly. It may feel as if you are looking at the space between your eyebrows, or the center of your forehead, the home of the "third eye." Many dowsers close their eyes and take a few deep breaths to center themselves before dowsing. When I do, my eyes naturally rise upwards as I think of making the connection to universal consciousness. It is a fluid, natural step that I no longer have to think about, and it automatically helps trigger the alpha state.

DOWSING AND QUANTUM PHYSICS

So now that we understand what is happening in a dowser's mind, let's look at the possible scientific explanations of how dowsing can work. The field of quantum physics has experienced dramatic advances in the past forty years or so. In 1964, Irish physicist John Bell started the momentum with Bell's Theorem, which has been called the most profound discovery in science. Bell established that two objects maintain a connection with each other long after they come apart, a *nonlocal entanglement*. Since then, laboratory experiments concerning the way photons interact when traveling away from each other at the speed of light have proved that nonlocality is real, and not, as Albert Einstein called it, "spooky action at a distance."

If we are all "entangled" in some way, could our focused attention on a question when we dowse enable us to pull in information regardless of time and space, like Leroy Bull does when he works on maps of remote locations?

Einstein himself believed in the authenticity of dowsing. In a letter to a friend, he wrote, "I know very well that many scientists consider dowsing as they do astrology, as a type of ancient superstition. According to my conviction this is, however, unjustified. The dowsing rod is a simple instrument which shows the reaction of the human nervous system to certain factors which are unknown to us at this time."[3]

Several other theories could explain how dowsing is possible. The first is the field theory, which suggests some kind of universal, nonlocal consciousness that we all can access—in other words, a boundless universal mind, unlimited by time or space. There's also the theory proposed by physicist David Bohm, which asserts that everything is entangled with everything else in a "holographic universe." When a "psi" event like dowsing occurs, could it be that we are accessing information from that holographic storehouse?

These theories and others have been suggested as possible explanations for psi, or paranormal, phenomena. Lynn McTaggart's *The Field* and Dean Radin's *Entangled Minds* both contain thorough descriptions of the current scientific understanding of psychic experience. If you are interested in the scientific research that has been done in this area, and how quantum physics is related, I highly recommend both books. As Radin explains, "Quantum theory is a mathematically precise and exquisitely well-tested description of the observable world. Psychic phenomena are slippery, subjective events with a checkered past. But as it turns out, the fabric of reality suggested by quantum theory and the observations associated with psychic phenomena bear striking resemblances. They are eerily weird in precisely the right way to suggest a meaningful relationship."[4]

There seems to be a direct relationship between states of higher consciousness, or focused intention, and the reality of the quantum world. Dowsers, as they pose questions and reach out to the cosmos for answers, have trained their higher consciousness to interact with the quantum world in a way that transcends time and distance. There is nothing supernatural about this, as Russell Targ explains in *Miracles of Mind*. Targ conducted groundbreaking experiments in psychic ability at the Stanford Research Institute, some covertly funded by the CIA. Dowsing is like the remote viewing that Targ describes in his book, "capabilities of what physicists have come to call our 'nonlocal mind.' This fascinating and not yet fully understood phenomenon that connects us to each other and to the world at large allows us to describe, experience, and influence activities occurring anywhere in space and time."[5]

As for studies of dowsing, the most concrete one to date was done by University of Munich physicist Hans-Dieter Betz, who explored dowsing as a means of finding water in Third World countries, and analyzed the data of two thousand drilled wells over a ten-year period.

"Unconventional Water Detection: Field Test of the Dowsing Technique in Dry Zones," financed by the German government and published in the *Journal of Scientific Exploration* in 1995, looked at the ability of dowsers to find underground drinking water in areas of arid terrain. Teams of dowsers and drillers were sent to ten countries, including Sri Lanka, Zaire, Kenya, Namibia, and Yemen. In Sri Lanka, a particularly difficult place to site wells, the dowsers advised drillers on the location of 691 wells with a 96 percent success rate. Geohydrologists doing the same thing had only a 21 percent success rate.

Unfortunately, Betz's experiments in the lab did not come close to his results in the field. He concluded that assessing dowsing in the lab was tricky at best. "The experiences gained from the Munich project have repeatedly revealed that certain artificial test situations ... do not yield notable success rates and, therefore, must be rejected as general qualifying tests for dowsers." In particular, he thought tests should be rejected if their sole purpose was to prove the existence or nonexistence of dowsing, especially if they were being conducted by "certain biased 'skeptics.'"[6]

Perhaps Betz was alluding to the million-dollar prize offered by the James Randi Educational Foundation (JREF) to anyone who can prove that dowsing is a true phenomenon.[7] The truth is that dowsing is nearly impossible to "prove" in a scientific experiment, because the human element leads to a certain amount of unpredictability. That said, there appears to be a wide disparity between those in the scientific community who are open to acknowledging that there is something going on with dowsing, but "we don't know what yet," and those who consider dowsing paranormal nonsense and want to debunk and dismiss it.

There are as many stories of dowsing successes as there are skeptics ready to discount them. But the goal of this book is not to prove that dowsing works or doesn't. My intention is to help you learn to focus your intention and learn to use your intuitive mind. If you master the states of higher consciousness necessary for dowsing, you will have immediate access to intuitive guidance whenever you need it—intuition in an instant. Dowsing is not the only way to get it, but I think it's one of the most direct routes.

3

Getting Started

The most important element in learning to dowse is to have an open mind. Go ahead and give yourself permission to dowse. Have a positive attitude and expect a good outcome.

Starting off on the right note is really that simple. We pick up all kinds of negative beliefs over the years from our religion, family, society, schooling, and more. You might have internal resistance, consciously or subconsciously, to the idea of opening your intuitive mind. So before you begin, give yourself full permission. It might be helpful to start off by removing any blocks or negative assumptions you might have by centering yourself and doing a clearing. This is a short meditation in which you ask your higher self for help in neutralizing anything that might stand in the way of your being able to dowse easily and accurately.

CLEARING BLOCKS TO DOWSING

Take a moment to quiet yourself. Sit comfortably in a chair with your feet on the ground and your hands in your lap or on your knees. Say to yourself or out loud, "I ask my higher self to examine my subconscious mind and remove any blocks keeping me from being 100 percent willing and able to dowse, and to dowse *accurately*." Then, because nature hates a vacuum, add, "Fill any space that is created with love and light."[1]

You may not need to do this clearing more than once. But if you find yourself having trouble as you work through this book, you can repeat this step. In the beginning, you may want to add it to your preparation and centering before each dowsing session.

DOWSING TOOLS

Most dowsers use a tool to help them amplify their dowsing responses—although, as we'll learn at the end of this chapter, it is possible to dowse using no device at all. Here's a roundup of the most common tools.

Pendulum

One of the easiest and most convenient dowsing tools is a pendulum. A pendulum (figure 3-1) is anything that can dangle in a balanced way from a string or chain. You can make one by slipping a ring on a chain, or a paperclip or shank button on some thread, or by tying a fishing weight to a piece of line. You can buy beautiful pendulums made from all different types of materials: crystals and semiprecious stones, metal, wood, and plastic. Typically, they are in an inverted triangle shape—bigger on top and tapering down to a point. The American Society of Dowsers bookstore has a wide selection of reasonably priced pendulums that can be purchased online (www.dowsers.org). You also can find them in New Age and metaphysical shops. If you can test them out in person, that's best because some will respond better for you than others. But if you have to order one online, the inexpensive wooden acorn pendulum at the ASD bookstore is a good one for beginners to try.

Pick up your pendulum and hold it in your dominant hand. Get comfortable with its weight and try giving it a slight swing. Hold the chain or thread fairly close to the pendulum—three inches is about right. You'll get a quicker response that way.

Put out your other palm and dangle the pendulum above it. I find that the energy from a person's hand

Figure 3-1: Pendulum

helps to activate movement in a pendulum. You can also try holding your pendulum over your knee. You should have both feet firmly on the floor, for grounding.

Next you'll need to "program" your pendulum, but that term can be misleading. You are not actually programming the pendulum; you are programming your mind to recognize your own *yes* response and *no* response. As I mentioned earlier, this can vary from person to person. My positive response is a clockwise spin and my negative response is a vertical swing up and down, but you might have a counterclockwise spin for yes and a diagonal for no, for example.

With your pendulum over your hand or knee, say, "Show me a yes." You can think this statement in your head, but I think it helps at first to say it out loud. Don't stare hard at your pendulum and try to will it to move. Instead, relax and expect to see the movement. Look at your pendulum with "soft eyes." In other words, relax your focus a bit and just concentrate on the statement, "Show me a yes." If you are still having trouble, try doing it with your eyes closed, and see whether you can sense movement in your pendulum. If so, open your eyes and see which way your pendulum is moving. If you still don't see any movement, try giving your pendulum a slight head start to get it moving. Pick a direction to program your yes response (clockwise, for instance), start your pendulum swinging in that direction, and tell yourself, "This is my yes." You are teaching your subconscious mind your yes response. Eventually, your pendulum will move in that direction without any help from you.

Once you have determined your signal for yes, repeat the procedure for no. If your pendulum is still moving in a positive direction, tell yourself, "Stop." It should come to a stop, or you can stop it with your hand. Now tell yourself, "Show me a no." Observe the kind of motion you are getting from your pendulum. Once it starts to move, you should see a swing that is very different from your positive one.

It can be helpful also to program a "maybe" response. Mine is a diagonal swing, and it helps alert me when the answer to my question is unclear, or there is a problem with the way I am asking it.

Once you have programmed your yes, no, and maybe responses, you can practice strengthening your connection. Figure 3-2 shows a circle crossed by diagonal, vertical, and horizontal lines. Feel free to draw your own diagram, or copy and enlarge the book version, if desired. Using only your mind, tell your pendulum to follow the lines: up and down, back and forth, sideways, and around in a circle.

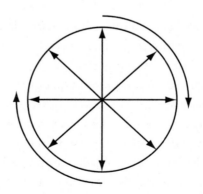

Figure 3-2: Circle of dowsing responses

You have just accomplished something amazing! You have managed to move something with your mind. Even the most die-hard skeptic is somewhat startled to feel the pendulum respond to his or her thought command. Of course, you aren't *just* moving it with your mind. Your body is making microscopically small movements in response to your directives. But you have programmed yourself to recognize your yes, no, and maybe responses. You have just calibrated a very sophisticated piece of scientific equipment: your brain. The magic isn't happening in the pendulum itself. That's why it makes no difference whether you are swinging an elegant crystal on a sterling chain or a Lifesaver candy on a piece of dental floss. The device is merely the tool, responding to the subtle energy readings of your brain.

When you ask a question and get an answer from your pendulum, or walk a field and detect the electromagnetic forces of the water veins beneath your feet with your L-rod, you are gathering information from outside of your five senses using a dowsing tool. But really, you are the tool. You are the energy detection device. Your pendulum is just amplifying the signals that you are picking up with your own brain.

If you are having trouble getting any kind of movement out of your pendulum, don't worry. Sometimes it takes a little longer to get comfortable with the whole concept. Practice for a short time every day. You might want to keep a pendulum in your pocket or on your nightstand. When I started, I practiced for a few minutes every morning. If you exercise regularly, you might want to try dowsing just after you have finished, when your energy levels are high. The more grounded you are, the better. Uncross your legs. Close your eyes. Clear your mind. Don't try to practice when you are getting sleepy in the evening. It's better to wait until you are fully awake. Also, if you've had alcohol or too much caffeine, you might find it hard to get accurate results.

Just keep at it. Practice and keep a positive attitude. Your goal is to connect with your intuitive mind. You can go back and do another clearing from time to time, chipping away at any hidden resistance you have to doing this kind of work. Make sure you are taking the time to center yourself and connect to universal energy.

Or, if you find you are still getting no response from your pendulum, try a different tool. You might respond better to L-rods or a bobber. In my classes, whenever someone is having difficulty with the pendulum, they are usually able to choose a different dowsing device and get immediate results.

Bobber

A bobber (figure 3-3) is a dowsing device with a fun attitude. I have one that has a wooden handle attached to a two-foot piece of wire, coiled at the base and weighted at the end with a small wooden ball. Basically, a bobber can be anything that is heavier on one end. Hold the lighter end in your hand and let the heavier end bounce or "bob" up and down. The first bobber I used was an old wire whisk that someone had twisted into the correct shape. I've watched an old-timer pick up a fresh tree branch that was heavier on one end and use that as a bobber. You can buy a bobber from the ASD bookstore, or you can try to make a simple one yourself.

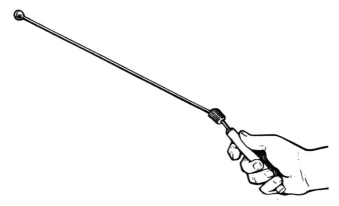

Figure 3-3: Bobber

Hold the bobber in your dominant hand and tell yourself, "Show me a yes." When I do that, the end of my bobber spins in a clockwise circle. Yours can move in a completely different way for both your yes and your no. Some people who find a pendulum difficult to use immediately discover that they like using a bobber. It just depends on your individual preference and comfort level. The only disadvantage to using a bobber is that it tends to be large and noticeable. Most likely, you will not be pulling out your bobber in public unless you want to attract a lot of attention. It's a lot easier to slip a pendulum in your purse or pocket than it is to cart around something that looks like a toy fishing pole.

L-Rods

L-rods (figure 3-4) are the dowsing device of choice for most water dowsers. They look like the letter "L." The short end of the letter is the handle and the long end acts like an antenna, pointing out ahead of you. You can easily make your own from coat hangers bent into an L-shape, or you can purchase a pair. Again, the American Society of Dowsers bookstore is a good source for these. L-rods come in lots of different varieties. Many people prefer the version with a "sleeve," a free-moving piece that covers the handle part of the L-rod. Your hands hold on to the sleeves and the L-rods move freely inside.

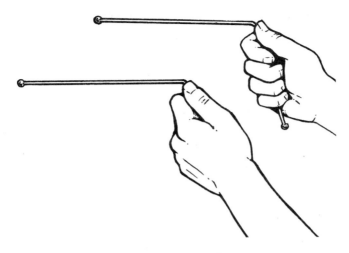

Figure 3-4: L-rods

But sometimes, they move a little too freely. When I first picked up a pair, they were swinging all over the place. Someone taught me to steady the rods with my thumbs at the top of the L—not enough to restrict their movement, but enough to calm them down and keep them in position. Hold them in your hands at chest height with your elbows tucked into your waist and your arms steady. The rods should point out ahead of you, with the long pieces on top parallel to the ground. Now tell yourself, "Show me a yes." The rods should swing into each other and cross. That is your positive response.

Since most people use L-rods in the field, they are just looking for a positive hit when they find something and don't require a no response. In other words, lack of movement in the rods is a negative response to a question. Or you can program yourself to get both a positive and a negative response from them. Crossing each other could be a yes, and swinging open could be a no. A partial cross, at a 45-degree angle, can be programmed as a maybe. If you find that your rods naturally fall open on a yes, that's fine, too. Establish that as your yes, straight ahead as your no, and the rods in the 45-degree-open position as your maybe.

Y-Rod

The classic image of a dowser is an old man in a field, walking around with a forked stick in his hands. In fact, the symbol of the American Society of Dowsers is a pair of hands gripping the ends of a Y-rod (figure 3-5). If you want to make one yourself, find a forked stick that is springy and strong. Branches of deciduous trees like witch hazel, beech, apple, and willow are good choices, but look around your back yard or in a park and see what you can find. Trim the stick so that each end of the Y is about eighteen to twenty-two inches. The ends should meet in the center, forming a tail that is four to six inches.

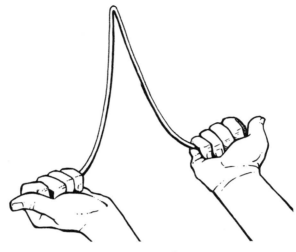

Figure 3-5: Y-rods

There are inexpensive plastic versions of Y-rods that you can buy, or you can improvise with what you have on hand. Bruce Irwin, a master water dowser in Athol, New York, teaches beginners to dowse using the half-inch-wide plastic binding straps that are cut off rolls of insulation at his local lumber yard. Grasp both ends of a two-foot length of the plastic strap and hold it so that the plastic makes an upside-down U. A yes response would cause the U to turn toward the floor. Similarly, if you grip both ends of the stick Y-rod, with the tail pointing up toward your forehead and your thumbs facing away from you, you are in the correct position. Tell yourself, "Show me a yes," and watch to see the tail tug downwards.

Body Dowsing

If none of these devices feels like the right fit for you, you might want to try body dowsing. This is a form of applied kinesiology that is used by alternative health professionals and others to test the energy of an internal or external situation. You may have heard the terms *muscle testing* or *energy checking*. This usually is done with one person holding their arm out in front or to the side, and another person pressing down on it. If they "stay strong" in testing a food substance or checking one of their energy meridians, the arm will remain straight. If they are "weak" in regards to what is being tested, the arm will move toward the floor.

Finger dowsing works the same way, except you don't need to rely on anyone else. There are several ways to do it. One is to make an O with your thumb and ring finger on both hands. Insert one O inside the other, or link them like a chain, and see whether you can break through the circle. If you can break through, you've tested "weak," or gotten your no response. If you "stay strong," you've gotten your yes. I like to do a variation of this by making the O with my left hand and sticking my right thumb inside the circle. If I break the circle, it's a no, and if the circle holds, it's a yes. Once you have gotten used to the correct amount of pressure to use, this can be very accurate. Test yourself by asking the question, "Is my name Kathryn?" substituting your name for mine. Play around with this until you get a yes response when you ask about your name.

There are other variations of body dowsing: standing upright and rocking back for a no and forward for a yes; keeping a steady gaze and interpreting a blink as a yes and no blinking as a no; rubbing your finger across a smooth surface and getting a smooth glide for a yes and a sticky, halting slide for a no.

I think it's best to start off using a dowsing tool to amplify your results, but if you are having trouble using a device, finger dowsing or another form of body dowsing can be a good alternative. Plus, it's nice to know how to dowse without a tool, because you will inevitably be somewhere without your pendulum or L-rods and have a need to dowse the answer to some pressing question. For the purposes of this book, I will generally direct you to use your pendulum, but feel free to substitute a different tool if you prefer.

Now that you've chosen which dowsing method you're most comfortable with, it's time to learn about the dowsing procedure.

PREPARATION AND CENTERING

Every dowser has his or her own ritual for dowsing. Some get in touch with the divine, source energy, or God. Some describe the act as "talking with my angels." For others, there is no spiritual connection at all. It's simply a matter of connecting with the intuitive mind and getting a response. How you choose to center and prepare yourself is a matter of personal choice. However, many people when dowsing like to think about connecting to a field of universal energy. Scientists have referred to this as the zero-point field. Others call it universal mind or the collective unconscious. Whatever name we place on it, it is thought to be a limitless body of energy that we can tap intuitively. Bruce Irwin, the master dowser in New York, calls it "the library in the sky."

To access it, simply imagine the connection. Visualize a column of light that shines from the top of your head to the cosmos, or a cord (like a telephone cord) that connects you to this body of energy. Place your feet firmly on the ground, and imagine that you are drawing up energy from the earth into the soles of your feet, all the way through your body. Now send that energy out the top of your head in a column of light that reaches out to universal energy. Take a few moments to imagine that connection. This visualization helps to ground you and to prepare your mind for intuitive work. When you start to dowse, make this a habit. Take a moment to close your eyes, clear your mind, and make the connection to universal energy. Your dowsing will become stronger and more accurate, and you will find it easier to connect to your intuitive mind. If, for whatever reason, you feel uncomfortable with the thought of connecting to universal energy, try connecting your higher self to pure truth.

Many dowsers start off by asking the questions, "May I? Can I? Should I?" These steps were outlined by a father of modern dowsing, Walt Woods, in his booklet *Letter to Robin*. They are part of what he calls "programs"—essentially, instructions to the subconscious. "May I? Can I? Should I?" basically means "Do I have permission to ask intuitive questions on this topic, do I have the ability to get the right answers, and is the timing right for me to check on this now?"[2]

Whether or not you choose to follow a dowsing program like this, checking in to see whether a topic is appropriate to dowse at that time is a good idea. It keeps us from delving into something that's not right for us to be examining for any number of reasons. We could be too ego-attached to it, or it could be unethical to pursue. So after centering yourself and preparing for dowsing, the first question to ask is, "Do I have permission to dowse about this subject at this time?" If the answer is yes, you can go ahead with your questions.

ASKING QUESTIONS

In dowsing, your results are only as good as the questions you ask. Try to make them as clear and unambiguous as possible. Instead of asking, "Is this vitamin good for me?" you might frame it as, "Is this vitamin what my body needs today?" When in doubt, I like to use the phrase "in my highest and best good." Is taking this new position in my highest and best good? Is booking that trip to Spain this summer in my highest and best good? Is taking an alternate route to work today in my highest and best good? It's not a perfect way of wording questions, but the phrase is a better substitute for the word "should." *Should* has so many negative connotations, it's best to avoid it when asking questions. If what first comes to mind is a "should I" question, try changing it to a question that starts off, "Is it in my highest and best good…"

Begin by asking questions that can be answered with a yes or no. Remember that your "maybe" response will help point out whether there is an issue with how you've worded the question. You can follow up by asking, "Is it best for me to ask the question in a different way?"

If you want to gather more information about the topic, you can try looking at it from a percentage point of view. In other words, if you get a maybe response to the question, "Is it likely to rain today in my neighborhood?" you could try asking, "What is the likelihood of it raining today in my neighborhood?" Hold that question in mind as you count slowly in your head from one to ten. Your pendulum will respond on the number that is the correct answer. If you get a positive swing on seven, the likelihood is 70 percent.

The percentage method can also be used in conjunction with a chart numbered from zero to one hundred (figure 3-6). This simple tool, known as a half-moon or half-circle chart, can be adapted to any question for which multiple answers are possible. Feel free to draw your own version of this diagram, or copy and enlarge the one in the book, if desired. Charts and lists are ways to get around the parameters of simple yes and no questions. We'll explore more of the specifics of charts and lists in other chapters of this book.

To use the percentage chart (figure 3-6), hold your pendulum over it and ask the question, "What is the likelihood of it raining today in my neighborhood?" It

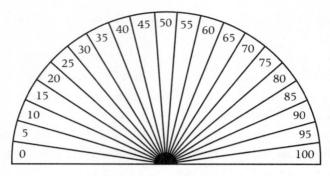

Figure 3-6: Percentage chart

will swing toward a number, indicating the chance of rain as a percentage.

So you've used your logical, rational mind (engaging the beta brain state) to formulate the question. That is only one part of the dowsing equation. Now you must step back and get into a detached, yet positive, mindset. This state has been shown to engage alpha brain waves, as we've seen in the last chapter. The dowser remains positive and hopeful, but unattached to any outcome or answer. If you find yourself *hoping* for a particular response, you will most likely interfere with the process and skew the results. It is critical to step back, detach from the outcome, and become an impartial observer. It's sort of like asking a question at a podium and then going back to your seat to wait for the answer.

STEPS FOR SUCCESSFUL DOWSING

1. Center yourself.
2. Check whether it's appropriate to ask questions about your topic.
3. Form your question.
4. Ask your question.
5. Detach yourself from the outcome and wait for a response.

If you get an answer you don't like, don't keep asking the question until you get the answer you want. Dowsing doesn't work that way. What you are doing, in essence, is telling your subconscious that you don't want to hear the truth. You can try rephrasing the question to get a more complete answer and possibly tease out additional data, but you run the risk of messing up the results. In general, your first response was probably the correct one.

Some dowsers say that if you are trying to get information about a problem in your own life, you may not get accurate results—so don't think of it as a *problem*. In your mind, let any outcome be okay. Pretend that you are dowsing the issue for someone else and let go of any emotion you might feel about the situation. Of course, that is more easily said than done.

There always will be issues that are difficult for us to dowse. Perhaps we are too attached to the outcome of a certain situation, or we are too involved somehow and it is hard to be objective. In those cases, one option is to have someone else dowse the question for you. Another option is to try dowsing the question "blind." Write down several questions on separate slips of paper. Be sure to include some that you can verify the answers to, so you will be able to gauge the accuracy of your dowsing. Fold up the pieces of paper, mix them up, and choose one at random. Dowse for your answer, make a note of whether the answer is yes, no, or maybe, and go on to the next.

Dowsing works best when you are searching for "what is" rather than "what will be." In other words, it's most effective to dowse for information about a situation or condition that presently exists rather than an event that may or may not happen in the future. Divination—attempting to foretell coming events—is a much more complicated and difficult process. There are too many variables, too many ways in which any situation may turn out. If you are moved to ask a question relating to a future event, try asking the question in a way that references the present: "Given the conditions that exist at this point in time, is it likely that this event will occur?" Or try to dowse the answer as a percentage, using the one-to-ten counting method or the percentage chart (figure 3-6): "How likely is it for this event to occur, given present conditions?"

The conventional wisdom among dowsers regarding asking about something in the future is that if you *need* the information, you will probably get it. In other words, if there's a clear reason for you to have advance knowledge of something, you will have a better chance at getting accurate information when you dowse. Just keep in mind that the answer you get is akin to a good guess. It's a snapshot of a possibility that exists in the future, given current conditions. Many variables can affect the outcome, so get a reading about a situation and then let it go. Often our inclination to ask questions about events in the future is driven by ego-based needs and attachments. If you have too much invested in the way you want something to turn out, make sure you check to see whether this is an appropriate topic to explore before you start dowsing about it.

ETHICS AND INTUITION

If you've followed the steps in this chapter, you've made amazing progress. You've learned to program your responses to subtle energy readings, and to focus your mind on a question and get into a detached intuitive state to allow the answer to come to you. Limitless information is available to dowsers, but here's the catch: we have to watch where we step. We can't go trudging through someone else's business just because we're able. Dowsing is not like getting a master key card to gain entry to every locked door in the world. Some doors we're not meant to walk through, at least not without an invitation, and being scrupulously ethical is essential in this field.

It's important to remember only to dowse within your sphere of influence. That basically means matters relating to yourself or topics that someone asks you to dowse for them. When in doubt, ask first whether it is appropriate and ethical for you to dowse on this topic. Your higher self will guide you.

One of the central concepts in dowsing, as in all intuitive work, is to trust yourself, and to trust that small voice inside you. Check in to make sure that any given topic is an appropriate one to explore. Stay within your own ethical boundaries and you will find that your intuitive voice will become stronger and you will naturally come to trust it more.

4

Kick-Start Your Intuition

Once you start accessing your intuition on a daily basis, your life will never be the same. You'll make decisions more confidently. Your insights into yourself and the people around you will improve. Goals will be easier to reach, and problems at work and at home will be resolved more quickly. You'll find yourself making choices that keep you in the flow, moving with the energy of a situation and not against it. Who wouldn't want that?

Becoming more intuitive can definitely change your life for the better. But before launching into all the ways that you can use the technique of dowsing on a daily basis, I'd like to talk more generally about intuition. Intuition is our birthright, a natural gift. We all have access to that inner voice, whether or not we have learned to listen to it. Like anything else, listening to it and using it become stronger with practice. If we practice quieting ourselves and asking for intuitive guidance, this "sixth sense" will grow stronger and more accessible in our lives. Your inner wisdom is waiting for you whenever you are ready for it.

"Quick and ready insight" is how Merriam-Webster defines intuition, or "the power or faculty of attaining direct knowledge or cognition without evident rational thought and inference." Intuition can take the form of knowing something will happen before it does (precognition), or interpreting signs, signals, feelings, or flashes of insight to perceive the truth of a situation. Using your intuition can mean sending your thoughts or feelings to another person (telepathy), or seeing a place in your mind's eye where you have never been before (remote viewing). Intuition can also involve working with energy and intention to effect changes that you want to happen, or to bring about healing.

But how many of us feel that we have "quick and ready insight" on demand, especially when facing important decisions? Before I learned to dowse, my intuition was not something I regularly called upon, except in a generalized "checking my gut" sort of way. Learning to dowse taught me to access my intuitive self in a systematic way. Now, whenever I need it, I have "intuition in an instant." I can get the answers I need, understand the truth of situations I find myself in, and ultimately make better choices.

This insight springs from a place other than our everyday, conscious mind. It comes from our subconscious mind and our highest self, the part of us that reaches out and touches everyone and everything. We are all one in this world of intermingling energy.

You can lead an intuitive life if you become accustomed to quieting your thinking brain and calling on your intuitive self. There are many, many ways to do that, but I have found dowsing to be one of the easiest and most practical methods. It gives you a visual indication that it is working, and what could be better than that? If you trust the process and practice it every day, I promise you that your intuition will grow stronger.

Sit with your pendulum right now and take a few moments to quiet your mind and let your breathing settle into long, deep breaths. Close your eyes, gently lift them as if to look at the center of your forehead, and imagine your higher self reaching out to the cosmos and connecting to universal energy and truth. Now open your eyes, pick up your pendulum, and ask if you are ready to engage with your intuitive self. You will likely get a healthy yes to this question. Yes, you *are* ready to engage with your intuitive self. You have just seen visual proof of your mind telling you that yes, you are ready. It doesn't matter what questions you ask today. It doesn't matter what answers you receive. Pick up your pendulum ten times, quiet your mind, and attempt to connect with your intuitive self. That simple process will reinforce the intuitive pathways. Do the same thing tomorrow. Pick up your pendulum ten times during the day for mini practice sessions. Let your pendulum become your friend. Let yourself become comfortable with the process of communicating with your intuitive self. We can nourish that process by practicing it every day and allowing it to become second nature.

As you go through this process, you may find that your intuitive gifts begin to blossom and expand. You may find it easier to interpret your dreams, for example, or you may see previously hidden patterns or symbols in your life. You may find there are more coincidences happening around you, or you may get a feeling that something is about to happen before it does. These are all signs that your intuitive self is answering your call to action. It is waking up and stretching. By practicing the technique of dowsing, you are actually telling your intuitive self, "I value the insights you have to share with me. I respect this gift. Please be more present in my life." Simply by asking for it, we become more intuitive.

This may be your first foray into trying to access your intuition, or you may have been at it for a considerable time. It makes no difference where you are on the journey. This is your own individual path toward growing wiser, toward seeing more. As you venture forward in exploring all aspects of your intuition, your dowsing technique can help. For instance, if you wake up remembering a vivid dream, jot down some notes and use your pendulum to help you decipher its meaning: "Was the bird a symbol of freedom? Do I want to be free of something or someone in my life?" Go through all the possibilities that occur to you while holding your pendulum in your hand. If you get no swing or a negative swing while asking a question, move on to the next. Your ability to do this will grow as your dowsing responses get quicker. I am so confident in sensing the movement of my pendulum now, I can tell which way it will swing almost before it starts.

If you use other intuitive tools, like tarot cards or rune stones, you can pick up your pendulum to help you interpret your readings: "Does this card represent what is going on with me and my boss, with whom I am currently having difficulties? What do I need to pay attention to in this card?" Perhaps it's not the meaning of the card as you know it. Maybe it is something in the background or in one of the minor details on the card— the butterfly taking flight, the movement of the clouds, the sun on the flowers. Use your pendulum to further explore the significance of that particular image.

Being more intuitive comes down to asking the right questions of yourself—sometimes many questions. Imagine all the things you might ponder in the course of a day. Should I take my usual route to work, or should I go the back way? This food has been in my refrigerator for over a week; is it safe to eat? What would be best to do today given my limited time: work on this project or swing by the library to get the book I need? I just watered that plant the other day, but it's wilting. Does it need more water or should I move it to another spot? Which room would be best? There are many ordinary, mundane decisions that you make each and every day. Try calling on your intuitive self to help make those decisions more quickly and effectively. Doing so on a daily basis will help strengthen those intuitive muscles, reinforcing the process that lets you quiet the thinking brain and discover your inner wisdom.

The next time you give your partner a backrub, try holding your pendulum over his or her back and asking, "What area needs the most attention?" When you get a positive spin, you can concentrate some of your efforts there, as you try to smooth out the muscle tension. You may want to rub your hands together to generate heat and bring energy into them. Then hold them over the spot you determined was best and send healing warmth to your partner.

If you want to make your creative visualizations more powerful, try incorporating your dowsing technique. First, get a clear vision of what you'd like to occur. Imagine it in the present, as if it is already happening. Call upon as many senses as you can to make your vision as clear as possible. Then hold your pendulum and ask it for a positive spin as you state your intention or goal. You may find that your pendulum spins very fast as you hold that thought. Continue holding your pendulum for as long as it spins. When it slows, relax your focus and put it down. Your pendulum acts as a visual manifestation of your focused energy. Your thoughts are powerful! Seeing your pendulum react to the energy of your intention may help you to hold your focus longer and achieve more.[1]

During a long car trip with a friend, we decided to raise the energy inside the car on the way home, so that we would arrive feeling more refreshed than when we started. We stated our intention as my pendulum swung wildly and continued to swing for several minutes. Ten hours later, we arrived at my friend's house and I helped get her things from the car. I was struck by how much better than usual my legs felt after a long drive. There was no cramping or heaviness down my legs. I even had enough energy to meet friends that night at my book group. Was it the intention that we set, amplified somehow by incorporating dowsing? I don't know, but I'll make sure to repeat the exercise before my next long car ride.

If you are a spiritual person, you may want to use your pendulum to deepen your intentions as you pray. You might ask if you have made the connection to your spiritual guide, or to whomever you pray. Then you can hold your pendulum as you say your prayer, allowing the swing to focus your thoughts on your intention, or you can use it to have a dialogue with your spiritual guide, asking questions and receiving answers from that source. If someone you love has passed away, you can use your pendulum to try to make a connection using the same technique. In essence, this is a form of mediumship; you are connecting with a soul who is no longer on this plane. This can be a deeply moving experience.

As you become more adept at calling on your inner wisdom through dowsing, you will inevitably find that your intuitive self disagrees with some of the decisions you make with your rational mind. If your logical, thinking self tells you one thing, but you get a different answer from your pendulum, take the time to look again at the situation. Often, errors in dowsing are the result of our thinking minds stepping in and swaying our results. We get the answer that our ego wants, rather than the correct answer. But when your ego (your rational mind) wants or believes something different from what your intuitive self says is true, pay attention. Consider the intuitive information as if someone you trust just told it to you.

Suppose you are considering what route to take to work. Your intuition tells you to go the back way—and your pendulum agrees—but your rational mind insists the main highway would be better. Listen to the traffic report to see if there's an accident on your normal route, and take some extra time to be aware. You may find that you still want to stick with your original decision. See how that plays out in your day. Did it take you longer to drive to work going the route you thought was best, when your intuition told you to go another way? Make a note so that perhaps, next time, your inner wisdom will win out.

As you call on your intuitive self more and more, you will find coincidences and synchronicities happening in your life with increasing frequency. You may have intuitive insights even when you don't pick up your pendulum and formally ask for guidance. By learning to dowse, you've opened the door to your inner wisdom.

5

Getting to Know Your Subconscious

Discovering secrets locked away in the subconscious is akin to unearthing buried treasure, and is just as valuable. These nuggets of truth can tell us so much about ourselves, and can help us navigate the paths we choose.

We each have a conscious, rational mind that runs our lives. It determines what choices we make in life, how we live, and what we do. But there is another, hidden part of ourselves, the subconscious, that is equally important. If your subconscious mind is in conflict with what your conscious mind is trying to do, you can expect to experience some difficulty. Not only does this inner conflict make it nearly impossible to make permanent changes, but the subconscious mind can try to get your attention using illnesses, accidents, fears, and anxiety. Deeply rooted blocks, false assumptions, and self-limiting attitudes can also arise from the subconscious.

The first step lies in understanding how the subconscious mind works. Then you can begin the process of untying these knots, releasing them and internalizing more accurate messages. I have found that people become stronger and more positive when these hidden blocks are released. Their personal energy increases, their intentions become more powerful, and even their dowsing becomes easier and more accurate. Dowsing is the perfect tool to "talk" to our subconscious mind and find out what's going on beneath the surface.

TALKING TO YOUR SUBCONSCIOUS

The subconscious is similar to your inner child. It is where emotions and memories are stored. All the thoughts, opinions, and judgments of your lifetime are gathered there, along with all the expectations and mores of society and religion. The subconscious takes care of the body, allowing all the physical functions to take place smoothly and without conscious thought. It likes pleasure and hates pain. It likes physical activity, walking, and sex, for instance, and dislikes right-brain activities like working on the computer or doing math.

The subconscious is very sensitive to negative messages, and yet most of us feed ourselves a daily dose of harsh, critical thoughts every day. Our bodies are not thin enough or toned enough. We are not smart enough or successful enough. When something goes wrong, we immediately think it's our fault. Those negative messages are exactly what our subconscious *doesn't* need. Instead, it needs to be nourished with kind, positive thoughts, and with thanks for doing such a good job.

I suggest that you get in the habit of talking to your subconscious on a regular basis, which will improve your dowsing ability as well as deepen your overall intuition. To do so, take a few moments to center yourself. You may want to sit in your favorite place for dowsing, if you have one.

Close your eyes and lift them slightly, as if you're looking at the middle of your forehead, to engage the alpha brain state, and take four deep, complete breaths. Take your time and allow yourself to inhale and exhale completely. Once you are in a relaxed state, hold your pendulum and ask if you can connect with your subconscious mind. If you get a positive result, you can continue. If you don't get a positive result, take some time to really think about how you're feeling. Are you anxious? Distracted? Pressed for time? The essence of connecting with oneself is being aware of your own emotions.

When I first started to get in touch with my subconscious, my pendulum swung in a counterclockwise circle to indicate a yes, as opposed to a clockwise circle as it usually does. My mind intuitively created a system so that I know when my subconscious is answering. That may not be the case for everyone, but you might want to experiment and see whether you can get a different positive swing when dowsing your subconscious.

Now, listening for an inner voice, ask yourself for the name of your subconscious. A name or a word might pop into your head. The gender of the name really doesn't matter here. If nothing comes to mind, you can use "Subbie" as a sort of nickname for your subconscious. If you receive a name, use your pendulum to confirm that this is the name your subconscious wants you to use.[1] Mine is called Betty.

In general, you may find it best to talk to your subconscious as if you were talking to a child or an adolescent. Be gentle and offer thanks for all the hard work it has been doing on your behalf. Then be quiet and ask what it is feeling. Something might come to mind quickly, an emotion or a thought. If you are having problems with a particular project or goal, ask your subconscious about it and use your dowsing skills to explore what's going on.

Recently, I was having difficulty writing an article and I couldn't understand why I was so unfocused. I spent a few minutes getting centered and then started a dialogue with myself. I asked Betty, my subconscious, "Do you want to work on this project?" I got a negative response from my pendulum. So I explored further by asking more questions. "Is it because you don't like the subject?" The answer came back no. "Are you afraid?" Again, that wasn't the reason. When I asked, "Is it because it is too much work?" I got a positive swing. Then I started trying to convince Betty that staying focused would actually make the work go much more quickly. I asked for her cooperation and struck a deal. If I could write for two concentrated hours first thing in the morning, I would make sure to take time for physical activity (something the subconscious likes) later in the day. My writing proceeded much more quickly, and I managed easily to meet my deadline.

Using your dowsing skills, you can find ways to be in agreement with your subconscious, and that will make your life flow much more easily.

WILLPOWER AND THE SUBCONSCIOUS

Many people get frustrated when they try, and fail, to make positive changes in their lives. They can't figure out why their plans are not working, even though they feel completely motivated and are consciously tapping their willpower to lose those twenty pounds, quit smoking, or find a new job.

What is the biggest obstacle to achieving your dreams? *You are*, if your subconscious is opposed to what you want to accomplish. Positive intentions, willpower, self-hypnosis, and visualizations all will fail if your subconscious resists the change you would like to make or the goal you hope to achieve. Dowsing enables you to actually dialogue with your subconscious and determine whether it's working with you or against you. This is critical when attempting to make changes in your life, but most people never consider it. If your subconscious doesn't want the change to happen, most likely it won't. Let me repeat that because it is so important: *you will not be successful in reaching your goal unless your subconscious is open to the idea.*

Any time you call upon willpower, you are using your logical, rational, conscious mind to set forward a new directive. You might want to lose weight or quit smoking. You might want to be more proactive at work or more confident in social situations. You might want to start an ambitious workout program. You will spend a lot of time thinking about your goal, perhaps drawing up a detailed plan that you can put into action. You tell yourself, "I can do this and I will do this. I will follow these steps and I will succeed." But there are many times when our best efforts are just not enough. Is it lack of willpower? Or are the rational and the intuitive sides of ourselves working against each other?

For example, try as you might to lose those last twenty stubborn pounds, you cannot do it. Why? Your unconscious self might be holding on to the weight. On a subconscious level, you may feel safer and more secure as a heavier person. Those twenty pounds could actually be a crucial protective layer, critical to your well-being—or so your subconscious thinks. This is why it is so important to dialogue with your subconscious: to find out what is actually going on. As a dowser, you have a distinct advantage. You can get in touch with the underlying motivations and beliefs of your subconscious simply by asking questions and using your pendulum.

Prepare as you would for any other dowsing session, but this time, make it your intention to connect with your subconscious self. Check to see whether you can ask questions of your subconscious at this time. If you get a positive response, you can proceed. Start by asking,

"Are there subconscious blocks to this goal I would like to achieve?" You can change the question as it fits your situation, and feel free to be specific. For instance, you could ask, "Are there subconscious blocks to my finding a different job?" or "Are there subconscious blocks to my quitting smoking?" If you get a positive response, you can then start a series of questions to explore the reasons behind the block: is it because you feel guilty, or unsafe, or undeserving, or you are protecting yourself, or you simply like things the way they are? Get as much information as possible to understand what is going on at the hidden, unconscious level.[2]

CLEARING A SPECIFIC BLOCK

If you determine that you have a block or an underlying motivation that is at cross purposes with what you would like to achieve, you will need to do a clearing to remove it. There are several ways to go about this, but the first and easiest approach is simply to ask. Call upon your higher self to assist you with removing whatever obstacles the subconscious has in relation to this goal. This is similar to the basic clearing you learned in chapter three.

Say out loud or to yourself, "I ask my higher self to examine my subconscious mind and remove any blocks that are preventing me from being completely willing to (state your goal). Fill the space that is created with love and light and whatever I need most at this time." Then dowse again to check and see whether the block remains.

SETTING YOUR INTENTION

Once you have removed the blocks from your subconscious, you can give yourself all the suggestions you want. You may think of this as self-hypnosis or setting a positive intention. Whatever you call it, you are replacing the old negative messages that were stored in your subconscious with the new positive script that you want to take its place.

First, spend some time thinking about your goal. How will your life be better when you achieve it? Write down several ways you can imagine your life improving. Visualize yourself when you have reached this goal. What pictures come to mind? Spend some time imagining a short video that stars you after you have accomplished your goal. Use all your senses to make the scene as rich as possible.

Take a few minutes to get centered and relaxed in your favorite dowsing spot. With your feet on the floor and your hands resting comfortably in your lap, close your eyes and take four deep, complete breaths. Now run the video again in your mind's eye. See it projected at about forehead level. If you want to use words to go along with it, be sure to keep it all in the present tense and keep the imagery positive. Rather than "I am no longer overweight," say, "I see myself at a healthy weight and physically fit. My clothes feel comfortable on my body, and I feel beautiful in them. I climb the stairs at work, and I have more energy than I can ever remember." Try holding your pendulum as you think or say your intention, as you learned in the last chapter. If it swings strongly, let it be a focus to hold your intention for the length of the swing.

You can also reason with your subconscious. "Subbie, you know that if we lose ten pounds, it will be much easier to work out and be active this summer. Our clothes will fit better and we'll have more energy after work to do the fun activities that we really enjoy. So are you open to going on this new diet?" At this point, dowse to see whether your subconscious has accepted the new plan. If you get a negative response, you can try using a more authoritative voice, or upping the emotion in the way you talk to yourself. Used by hypnotherapists, these techniques can impress upon the subconscious the importance of what you are trying to do.

REMOVING NEGATIVE ASSUMPTIONS

For many of us, deep-seated beliefs and false negative assumptions in our subconscious keep us from leading an optimal life. Sometimes the things we are telling ourselves at the subconscious level seem shocking when they are revealed to us: "I feel guilty." "I can't forgive myself." "I don't deserve it." "I am not lovable."

You can dowse to discover these underlying emotional states and/or negative assumptions either by going down the list holding your pendulum in your dominant hand and pointing at each word with a pencil in the other, or by using a circle chart. A circle chart is similar to the half-circle chart you learned about in chapter three, but its larger size allows for more flexibility and more potential answers. Figure 5-1 is an example of a full-circle chart that you can redraw or photocopy, adding in lists of possible answers. You can create a larger or smaller chart,

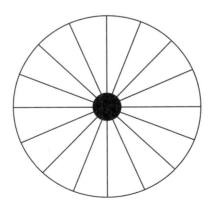

Figure 5-1: Full-circle chart

depending on how many potential answers you can come up with. Throughout the remainder of the book, several lists of words are provided that can be assigned to different segments of the circle chart and then used as you seek your answers.

List of underlying emotions

Abandonment

Anger

Anxiety

Betrayal

Bitterness

Blame

Controlling

Denial

Depression

Don't deserve

Easily influenced

Emotionally distant

Envy

Fearful

Greedy

Guilt

Hate

Hurt

Insecurity

Jealousy

Lack of courage

Lack of trust

Low self-esteem

Misunderstood

No self-love

Not nurtured

Not protected

Not supported

Other

Rage

Resentment

Revenge

Self-loathing

Self-punishment

Shame

Uncompassionate

Unforgivable

Unforgiving

Unloved

Unsafe

Unworthy

Victim

Settle into your favorite dowsing place and center
yourself. Close your eyes, raise them to forehead level to

engage the alpha brain state, and take four deep, complete breaths. Now reach out to your subconscious and ask it to reveal what it believes to be true. Open your eyes and, holding your pendulum at the center, dowse over the chart. Keep your mind open. Don't try to judge or reject what your subconscious is telling you. Your pendulum may move to more than one statement, and it may swing more forcefully on one that's particularly important. Once you know which "truths" are pertinent, you can ask more questions about each one to find out exactly how it is affecting you. You can use the percentage chart (figure 3-6) to get a sense of the magnitude of the problem, and the body chart (figure 5-2) to learn whether the problem is manifesting on a physical, emotional, spiritual, mental, or karmic level. For example, if you are exploring the response "rage" from figure 5-1, and you receive the response "karma" from figure 5-2, you can conclude that your unconscious anger has a past-life component.

After you have gathered information about your subconscious blocks, you can remove them with a specific clearing, which you learned earlier in this chapter. After you have done so, dowse again to check and see whether the block remains. If it does, I suggest that you talk with your subconscious self and present a logical, reasonable case for why that statement is false. For example, some-

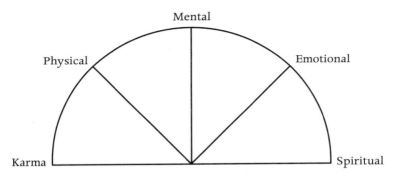

Figure 5-2: Body chart

one who feels she doesn't deserve the success she's experienced might say to her subconscious, "We *do* deserve all the good we have in our life. We have worked hard to achieve our goals. I am a good person and always try to do my best." Then dowse to see whether the subconscious is now ready for a clearing, and repeat the process.

Understanding what is going on inside the subconscious mind is a good place to start dowsing, because the process helps to remove blocks to our intuition. The clearer we are, the more accurate our dowsing will be. This journey begins with self-knowledge, and can make us wiser and more self-aware. It can also make us healthier. So now that we've looked at dowsing as a way to explore the mind, let's look at how it can give us information about what's happening inside the body.

6

Dowsing for Health
and Healing

We make scores of decisions every day on matters relating to our health, whether we realize it or not. The foods we put in our bodies, the vitamins we take, even the water we drink, all impact how our bodies feel and function.

When we are dealing with illness, getting well is our highest priority. That's when we are most intensely focused on every choice we have to make. A doctor may prescribe one of several medications that would work for a particular problem, or suggest some over-the-counter alternatives. Which one would be best for you? He or she may recommend surgery for a minor issue. Would it be best to schedule that now, or wait to see if the condition resolves itself? You feel sluggish and weak. Is it a vitamin deficiency, or are you coming down with the flu?

You probably have been relying on your gut instinct your whole life to help you make these decisions. Now, with dowsing, you have the skills you need to be your own intuitive health consultant. Of course, you should always talk with your doctor before making any important decision regarding your health. But having the ability to get guidance on an intuitive level adds a degree of confidence to the process. Think of it as getting another opinion, much as you would get a second opinion from another doctor when considering surgery. You wouldn't necessarily follow the opinion of the second doctor if he (or she) completely disagreed with your primary physician. But it would increase your confidence if he agreed, and make you think twice if he didn't.

Anyone who has spent any time dealing with a serious health issue knows that it is prudent to be your own best advocate. No one cares more about your health than you do. Asking questions relating to your health with your pendulum can give you access to inner wisdom to help your body function at its best.

PREPARING TO DOWSE

Before you dowse on any health topics, check to make sure you don't have any blocks or obstacles that would hinder your accuracy. Sit in your favorite dowsing spot, center yourself, and take four deep, complete breaths. Say to yourself, "I ask my ego to step aside. I ask my higher self to connect to the source of universal energy and wisdom. I ask to connect to what is true, what is real, and what is in my highest and best good."

Now open your eyes and pick up your pendulum. Ask whether you have any blocks that could keep you from accurately exploring questions relating to your health. If you don't have any, confirm that you can ask questions on this topic at this time, and then proceed. Remember, you are connecting to "what is in your highest and best good," *not* to your subconscious mind as we did in the last chapter.

If you do get confirmation that you have a block or obstacle, you'll need to ask your higher self to help you remove it before continuing. Sometimes we have attachments to certain issues, or the ego holds on to a certain outcome, and that can make it harder for us to get accurate answers when dowsing, particularly where health matters are concerned. It's as if the "filter" between our questions and our inner wisdom becomes thicker. Answers can become skewed. If you know that your health dowsing is problematic, take that fact into consideration when making important decisions. Weigh information obtained through your dowsing as you would that from any other source. If someone in a health food store recommended an herbal supplement, would you take it without doing any research? I wouldn't, and I also wouldn't take any supplements that I learn are good for me, through dowsing, without finding out more about them. If dowsing on health issues presents an ongoing challenge for you, I suggest having a friend dowse the question for you instead.

Vitamins and Supplements

I'd like you to try an experiment right now. Take out all the vitamins you have in your cupboard and line them up on your counter. Pick up your pendulum and ask yourself which vitamin your body needs at this time.

Remember to center yourself, as always, take four deep, full breaths, and connect to universal energy and truth. Start with a general question: "Which of these are in my highest and best good to take today?" Then hold your pendulum over each bottle and see which ones get a response. It's interesting to try this blind, without looking at the labels, so that you don't know which vitamin you are dowsing. I once tried this experiment with some herbal tinctures that were all in identical bottles. I was amazed that the only bottle I got a hit on was the one formulated to fight a cold, which I was suffering from at the time.

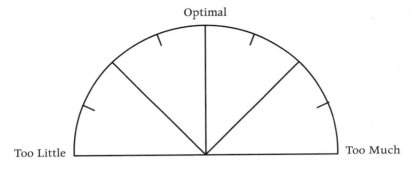

Optimal

Too Little

Too Much

Figure 6-1: Optimal chart

Once you have narrowed down your vitamin bottles, you can refine your questions further: "Is it in my highest and best good to take all of these today?" You may find that if you take a multivitamin, you should not take an additional supplement. In other words, if you are low in vitamin B, just taking your multivitamin might be enough to correct the deficiency, and you may not need to take the extra B-complex. Or you might find the opposite to be true.

Another way to check on your vitamin usage is with the optimal chart (figure 6-1). This is another half-circle chart, intended to show the effectiveness of your dosage. Ask yourself, "Am I getting too little of this vitamin, just the right amount, or too much?" Hold your pendulum at the base of the chart. A vertical swing straight up and down over the chart would show that you are getting the optimal level of the vitamin in question. To the left is too little, and to the right is too much. Pay attention to where your pendulum swings. Very close to the baseline in either direction indicates an extreme: way too little, or way too much. Feel free to draw your own version of the chart, or copy and enlarge the one in the book, if desired.

Another technique is to use the percentage chart (figure 3-6). Ask yourself, "How much vitamin C have I been getting over the past two weeks?" Hold your pendulum over the chart and see where the swing falls. A straight up and down swing would put you at the 50 percent mark. You are taking in only half the vitamin C that is optimal for your body at this time.

If you are not comfortable using a pendulum and prefer a bobber, rod, or body-dowsing method, you can still ask these questions, but in a different way. Pick up a pencil to use as a pointer. While holding your bobber or rod in one hand and the pencil in the other, ask yourself, "How much vitamin C have I been getting in the past two weeks?" Move the pencil to each section of the chart until you receive a positive response.

If your dowsing technique requires two hands, simply hold the question in your head instead. You can ask whether your intake of each vitamin over the last two weeks has been low, just right, or high. Or use the counting method, counting from one to ten to give you the correct proportion.

When you go to the store to buy your vitamins and supplements, you may want to bring your pendulum along. I often find that there is a difference in the various formulations, and that one brand usually stands out from the others as being better for me.

FOODS

One of the most helpful ways to use dowsing for your health is to determine whether you are eating an optimal diet. First, go through the list of foods holding your pendulum in your dominant hand and pointing at each word with a pencil or chopstick in your other hand. If you find it easier to use a chart, you can make several copies of figure 5-1 in the book, and write in the food items. Hold your pendulum in the center of the circle chart and ask yourself what foods you should limit.

List of Foods
    Acidic foods
    Aged cheese
    Alkaline foods
    Bacon, processed meats
    Barley

Beans, legumes, peas

Berries

Butter

Carrots

Celery

Chocolate/Cocoa

Coffee

Corn

Cow's milk

Eggs

Fish

Food coloring

Fresh cheese (mozzarella, goat)

Fruits

Garlic

Meats

Nightshade vegetables (eggplant, tomatoes, potatoes, peppers)

Nuts & Seeds

Oat

Oils

Onion

Poultry

Preservatives, sulphites

Processed cheese

Rice

Shellfish
Soy milk
Soy products
Spelt
Spices
Sugar
Tea
Vegetables
Wheat products
Yeasted breads
Yogurt/kefir

Hold your pendulum at the bottom center of the chart and ask yourself what foods you should limit. There may be more than one item, and your pendulum may move quickly from one to another. If the swing is dramatic on a particular item, you may have a problem with that food. Once you know what your problem areas are, you can explore them further.

Next, using the list of foods again, ask yourself which foods are best for you to avoid altogether, or which contribute to food sensitivities or allergies. If something like fruit comes up as a potential problem, make a list of all the fruits that you know, even ones that you don't eat on a regular basis. Now, using a pencil or a chopstick as a pointer, go down the list pointing at each one, and ask for a positive spin on which ones you should avoid. This can be an effective way to get extremely precise information on the diet that's best for you at this time.

Dowsing a list of terms is an easy alternative to drawing a circle or half-circle chart. First decide on your question, then make a list of all the potential answers. As in the above example, go down the list with the pencil in your nondominant hand and your pendulum in your dominant hand. Point at each term with the pencil and ask your pendulum for a positive response on the accurate answer or answers.

If you are comfortable dowsing in public, you can dowse as you look at a restaurant menu, or in a buffet line, or over an actual plate of food. I often use the finger-testing method when it's not convenient to pull out my pendulum. Just remember to connect to universal energy to dowse what is in your highest and best good. If you don't, you may connect with your subconscious, which has its own agenda. The subconscious veers toward pleasure and away from pain, after all. So chocolate could come up as a food your body *needs*, when in reality it is what you *crave*.

Keep in mind that dowsing, like anything else in life, can be taken too far. Don't get so carried away with dowsing that you feel the need to check with your pendulum about everything you put into your mouth. But every so often, reviewing your diet and the supplements your body needs can be a helpful, and sometimes surprising, endeavor.

MEDICAL INTUITION READINGS

After dowsing successfully for several years, I felt drawn to do intuitive health readings and I had no idea why. Without any kind of medical background, I had no reason to think I would be accurate in any way. But the guidance I kept getting told me to start.

I called my friend Jane and told her what I wanted to do. "Think of someone you know who is ill," I told her, sketching a rough outline of the human body on a sheet of paper. "Hold that person in your mind and I'll dowse for him or her." I held my pendulum over my drawing, moving it slowly over the head and torso, down the arms and legs, watching for it to respond. "Well, I got a spin on the left foot, the groin, and the lower torso. Is that right?"

There was a big pause before she replied, "He has diabetes and stomach cancer, and the diabetes is severely impacting his left foot."

We both were slightly shocked. Could it be so easy to tap into the medical conditions of people I had never met? What else could I discover about my own body, about conditions I had, as well as those that had yet to surface?

I want to emphasize that dowsing in this manner is *not* a medical diagnosis, and anyone presenting a psychic reading as such is completely unethical. The American Society of Dowsers publishes a statement of policy on healing in each quarterly issue of *The American Dowser*, directing staff to "reject all requests of a medical nature, either directly or for referral to a member or chapter."

That said, your intuition can be an amazing resource for you and your loved ones, and a personal medical reading can go into as much detail as you desire. Make a copy of the health sheet in figure 6-2 on pages 92–93 and write the name of the person you are dowsing for at the top. As you would when accessing your inner wisdom on any topic, take a few minutes to center yourself and connect to your higher self. Inquire first whether it's okay to ask questions about this topic for yourself, or for someone else. If you are dowsing for someone else, ask your ego to step aside so that you can be a clear, open channel for that person. In other words, you are the conduit. I like to think of myself as the telephone line. I may not know much about medical conditions and treatments, but I can be a clear, strong connection to universal consciousness, where many answers lie.[1]

Hold your pendulum over the drawing of the body and move it slowly up and down. If you find that you get a spin anywhere, draw a circle at that spot. After you have gathered all the information you can from the body chart, answer the questions: Is the problem related to what the person is doing, not doing, overdoing? Is the problem urgent or not critical? Add that information to the sheet.

Now, go down the list of organs and systems of the body using the method explained in the previous section for dowsing a list or using a circle chart. Ask the question, "What do I need to pay attention to? Show me areas of disturbance." Then point to each term with a pencil in your nondominant hand as you hold your pendulum in your dominant hand. Note any hits on your sheet under "Disturbances."

Systems of the Body

Abdomen
Adrenals
Ankles
Anus
Appendix
Arms
Arteries
Bladder

Name: _____

Date: _____

Allergies/Foods to Avoid:

_____

_____

_____

_____

_____

Supplements:

_____

_____

_____

_____

_____

Disturbances:

_____

_____

_____

_____

_____

_____

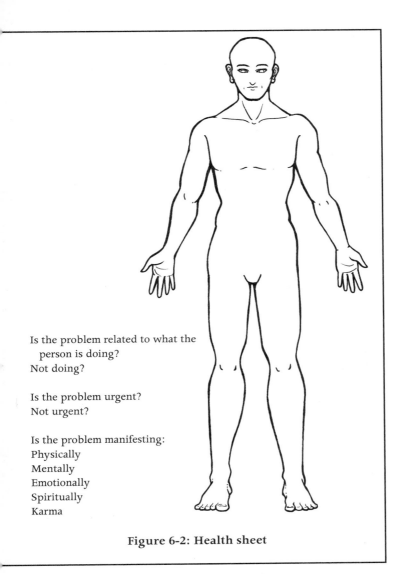

Is the problem related to what the
person is doing?
Not doing?

Is the problem urgent?
Not urgent?

Is the problem manifesting:
Physically
Mentally
Emotionally
Spiritually
Karma

Figure 6-2: Health sheet

Blood

Blood pressure

Bones

Bowels

Brain

Breast

Capillaries

Cartilage

Cells

Central nervous system

Colon

Diaphragm

Ears

Esophagus

Eyes

Fallopian tubes

Feet

Fingers

Gall bladder

Genitals

Groin

Gums

Hands

Head

Heart

Hips

Hormone system

Hypothalamus

Immune system

Intestines

Joints

Kidneys

Knees

Legs

Ligaments

Liver

Lungs

Lymph glands

Mammary

Metabolism

Mind

Mouth

Muscles

Nails

Neck

Nerves

Neurological system

Ovaries

Pancreas

Parathyroid

Parotid glands

Pelvis

Penis

Pharynx

Pineal

Pituitary

Prostate

Rectum

Respiratory system

Ribs

Shoulders

Sinuses

Skin

Spine

Spleen

Stomach

T-cells

Teeth

Tendons

Testicles

Throat

Thymus

Thyroid

Tissues

Toes

Uterus

Vagina

Veins

Vertebrae
Wrists
Other

Next, refer to the half-circle chart showing common allergies (figure 6-3). Hold your pendulum at the bottom center of the chart and ask, "What substances is this person sensitive to? What should be avoided?" If the person you are dowsing about is having an allergic response but can't pinpoint the cause, ask, "What is causing this problem?" You also may want to check for the presence of food sensitivities (use the list of foods on pages 85–87) and supplements that may be needed (figure 6-4). Note all the responses on your copy of figure 6-2.

Doing a medical intuition reading is a snapshot in time. It can draw your attention to conditions you may not be aware of, or point you toward courses of treatment that could be helpful. Checking in on a regular basis is a good idea, because our bodies are always changing.

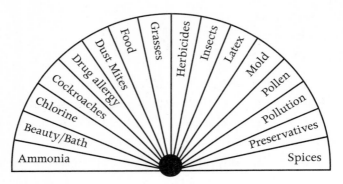

Figure 6-3: Allergy triggers

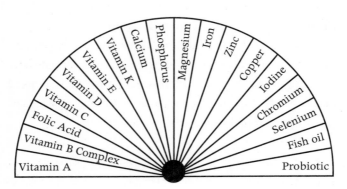

Figure 6-4: Supplements chart

7

The Energy Body: Balancing the Chakras

A chakra is an energy center in the body, and you have seven major ones. The word comes from Sanskrit and means "turning" or "wheel," since the energy in each chakra rotates or turns. Our knowledge of chakras comes from the yogic tradition, dating back thousands of years. The first mention of chakras is found in the Vedas, the oldest religious texts of India.

Our chakras take in energy from our environment, like a funnel pulling in energy from the universe, and also radiate energy out. When harmonized and balanced, our chakras contribute to our physical and psychological well-being. When there is an imbalance with our chakras, we may experience health problems or emotional upsets.

The aura is an invisible energy field that surrounds all living things, separate from but related to the chakras. I have found that people with strong, positive dispositions have larger energy fields that extend up to three feet away from their bodies. People who are going through difficult times, or who are experiencing some kind of health challenge, have smaller energy fields that may extend only about a foot from their bodies.

BODY ENERGY AND DOWSING

For years, I talked about a person having "good energy" without really knowing what I was saying. Of course, I had heard about auras and chakras. I knew in theory that we all have an energy body that surrounds us, but it wasn't until I picked up a pendulum and held it a foot or so from my heart that I was convinced. My spinning pendulum showed me how real and concrete my chakras are, and it gave me valuable information about their condition, whether they were open or closed, whether they were hindered in some way or flowing strongly. It's almost like throwing a dusting of powder into light streaming in through a window. What is not visible with the naked eye becomes clear.

Something similar happened when I tried to determine how far a friend's aura extended. My girlfriend and I each held our pendulums and walked toward another friend without looking at each other. We were stunned as our pendulums started spinning at the exact same moment, at the exact same distance from our friend. We had both hit the edge of her energy body and it was as clear as if we had hit the edge of a physically tangible thing.

Try it yourself. Work with a friend and try to determine the range of his or her energy field. Tell yourself that you want to see a positive response when you hit the edge of the aura. Stand a good distance away. I like to move to the far end of the room, and I hold the pendulum away from me so as not to pick up on my own energy field. Now slowly start walking toward your friend, holding the thought in your head, "Show me the outer edge of his energy field." You will definitely recognize it when you reach it.

If you have a friend who knows how to dowse, try the experiment together with another friend as your "target." Stand at least six feet apart, but the same distance away from the target. Then walk in slowly, keeping an eye on your pendulum, not on each other. Call out when you get a hit. You will be amazed to find that your pendulums spin at exactly the same time.

Even skeptics who have trouble believing that any accurate information can be pulled in from universal consciousness seem to easily accept this experiment when they've witnessed it. An energy body or aura does exist around each of us, and a pendulum can show you its contours. Again, what is the definition of dowsing? To get information outside of the five senses. Using dowsing in this way, to see what is not visible to the naked eye, is doing exactly that.

GETTING TO KNOW YOUR CHAKRAS

Start by using your pendulum to learn where your chakras are located. Hold your pendulum in front of your body at the level of your heart, about six to ten inches away from you. Hold the thought in your mind, "Show me where my chakras are." Wait until you get a positive response at your heart chakra, then slowly move your pendulum lower. It should stop spinning once it's away from your heart chakra. Stop lowering it when it resumes moving in a positive swing. You should find your solar plexus chakra just above the navel, the sacral chakra just below the navel, and the root chakra at your lower pelvis. Return back to the heart level and slowly begin to move your pendulum higher. You should locate your throat chakra at the base of your neck, your third-eye chakra in the center of your lower forehead, and your crown chakra at the top of your head.[1]

Since each chakra is associated with a specific area of the body (see figure 7-1), chakras provide a way to gain valuable information about what is going on inside you. Asking the question, "Which chakra needs attention?" is the first step. Move your pendulum in front of each of your chakras, starting at your root chakra and ending at the crown chakra. (Note that you can also use the chart in figure 7-1 to scan your own chakras, or those of someone else, similar to the medical intuition reading in chapter six. Feel free to draw your own version, or copy and enlarge the one in the book, if desired.)

When you get a positive spin for a particular chakra, ask, "Is this chakra balanced? Is it under-energized, or over-energized?" Once you have answers to these questions, ask, "How is the imbalance showing up in my life?" Use the half-circle chart in figure 5-2 to determine whether the imbalance is manifesting on a physical, emotional, spiritual, mental, or karmic level. If you learn that the imbalance is primarily physical, use the body chart in figure 6-2 or the list of body parts on pages 91–96 to further pinpoint the affected locations. Finally, ask, "What is the best method of balancing this chakra?" Use the half-circle chart, figure 7-2, which lists some healing modalities: meditation, energy work, yoga, aromatherapy, sound therapy, gemstones, color therapy, exercise, dance, reiki, or past-life clearing.[2]

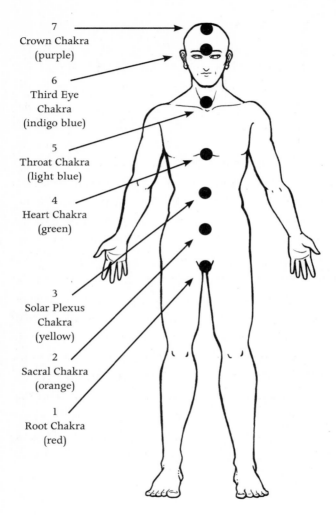

7
Crown Chakra
(purple)

6
Third Eye
Chakra
(indigo blue)

5
Throat Chakra
(light blue)

4
Heart Chakra
(green)

3
Solar Plexus
Chakra
(yellow)

2
Sacral Chakra
(orange)

1
Root Chakra
(red)

Figure 7-1: The chakras

The Crown Chakra is located on the top of the head and honors Spiritual Connectedness. Associated with spirituality, cosmic consciousness, and higher planes.

The Third Eye Chakra is located in the center of the forehead and honors the Psyche. Associated with intuition, imagination, and self-knowledge.

The Throat Chakra is located at the throat and honors Communication. Associated with self-expression and communication.

The Heart Chakra is located in the center of the chest and honors the Heart. Associated with love, empathy, compassion, and openness.

The Solar Plexus Chakra is located at the solar plexus, below the diaphragm, and honors the Life Force. Associated with who we are in the world, purpose, will, and spontaneity.

The Sacral Chakra is located just below the naval and honors the Creative. Associated with sexuality, creativity, and emotions.

The Root Chakra is located at the base of the spine and honors the Earth. Associated with stability, being grounded, trust, and safety.

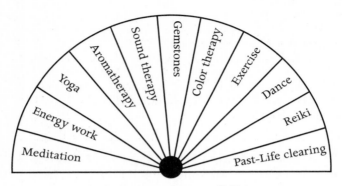

Figure 7-2: Healing modalities

Healing modalities

Meditation

Energy work

Yoga

Aromatherapy

Sound therapy

Gemstones

Color therapy

Exercise

Dance

Reiki

Past-life clearing

An improperly balanced chakra can affect its associated body parts, as well as a range of related emotions.

For example, the throat chakra is located at the base of your neck and is associated with the color light blue. If it is closed and needs opening and balancing, you might be feeling stifled in communicating with others, unable to tell your "real" story, or afraid to tell the truth. In addition, many people believe that blocks in the energy body can have their roots in past-life experiences, so perhaps you were unable to "speak your truth" in a past life, and the subconscious memory of that experience is affecting your throat chakra now. And finally, since the throat chakra is associated with the thyroid, you might also want to check with your doctor to determine whether the problem you are having with a closed chakra is related to a physical condition. Some healing strategies for a throat chakra imbalance include primal screaming, singing, and chanting.

The gentlest way to address an imbalance of any chakra is simply to send love to that energy center. Hold your hands in a cuplike fashion over the chakra and imagine healing light and love streaming in from the universe. Ask the universe to "send this chakra what it needs at this time." A great deal of information about chakras and the energy body, including techniques for balancing chakras, can be found on the Internet.

Perhaps you didn't get a positive spin from your pendulum when asking the question, "Which chakra needs attention?" If that's the case, you've learned that your chakras are open, balanced, and flowing freely. The following meditation can help keep them functioning properly.

CHAKRA MEDITATION

This meditation is a gentle way to harmonize your chakras. It can be done on its own, or added to your regular meditation practice.

Take a few moments to center yourself. Close your eyes and take four deep breaths in and out. In your mind's eye, imagine a red circle of energy spinning clockwise, centered at your pelvis. Spend a few minutes focused on the glowing red color of your root chakra. Actively send love to this area, and ask that it be balanced. Hold the thought in your mind, "I am safe and secure. My body is grounded. I am rooted in the earth."

Next, move your focus to your sacral chakra, located just below your navel. See in your mind's eye a circle of vibrant orange energy. Take a few minutes to focus on it, and see and feel it spinning clockwise. With each inhaled breath, send love to your sacral chakra and ask that it be balanced. Hold the thought, "I deserve and enjoy pleasure in my life. I create easily and effortlessly."

Move next to the solar plexus chakra, located just above your navel, and see in your mind a circle of radiant yellow energy. Again, imagine the circle spinning clockwise while you send love to that area. Ask the universe to balance your solar plexus chakra, and hold the affirmation, "I feel the power within me. I accomplish what I set out to do."

Now move to your heart chakra, in the center of your chest, and see a circle of vivid emerald green energy in your mind's eye. Imagine the circle spinning clockwise while you send love to this area and ask for balance. Think to yourself, "I give and receive love. I love easily and freely. I forgive myself and I forgive others."

Move your awareness to the throat chakra, located at the base of your throat. Imagine a circle of brilliant turquoise blue energy and see it spinning clockwise. Breathe in and out slowly as you focus on sending love to your throat chakra. Ask the universe for help in balancing this area as you hold the thought, "I express myself clearly. I hear and speak the truth."

When you are ready, bring your attention to your third-eye chakra and imagine a circle of luminous deep blue or indigo energy. See it spinning clockwise as you send it love and ask for balance. Focus on your breath, breathing in and out slowly for a few minutes. While you do so, think to yourself, "I trust my intuition. I call on the wisdom within." Finally, move to your crown chakra at the top of your head. Imagine a circle of dazzling purple energy spinning clockwise as you breathe deeply. Send love to your crown chakra and ask that it be balanced. Focus on the thought, "I am open to spiritual guidance. I honor the divine within."

Now slowly move through the glowing colored circles again as you imagine them spinning in harmony. From the purple crown chakra, move to the indigo circle at your third eye, the turquoise circle at your throat, then to the green circle at your heart, the yellow circle at your upper belly, the orange circle just below your navel, and the red circle at your pelvis. All your chakras are perfectly balanced. You are energized. Divine love and light flow freely through you. To finish, return once more from the root chakra to the crown, pausing briefly on each colored circle to see it in your mind's eye, feel its gentle spinning, and sense its color. When you feel ready, open your eyes.

After you have completed the meditation, use your pendulum to once again scan your chakras. Hold it in front of each one and ask, "Is this chakra balanced?" Are the responses you receive now different than previously?

Healers claim there are many benefits of working with your energy body. They say you may be able to heal circulatory problems, boost your immune system, help your body detoxify, stimulate digestion, and get better sleep. You can diminish anxieties, mood swings, and depression. You can promote inner peace and positive thinking, and gain insight into your true purpose in life.

It almost sounds too good to be true. But what if simply checking in with our energy body on a regular basis gave us the key insights we needed to maintain optimal health? What if doing a basic chakra meditation helped keep our energy centers balanced and flowing? There is no downside to intuitively checking our chakras and making sense of the information we find. Dowsing, with its ability to amplify the vibrations of the energy body, is the perfect tool to help us learn the language of the chakras.

8

Exploring Relationships with Dowsing

Just as intuition can give us important insights into ourselves, it can also shed light on our relationships with others. What does our loved one want and need? Is this a relationship I want to pursue? What was the real reason behind that blowup? How can we live more harmoniously?

Internet dating was a scary proposition for Liza, a forty-six-year-old widow with two kids. But once she narrowed her choices down to a few men whose profiles she found interesting, Liza relied on her intuition to help screen her dates. "Is contacting this person in my highest and best interest?" she asked. If she got a yes response with her pendulum, Liza would send him an e-mail.

She was puzzled when some dates turned out to be completely wrong for her. Was her dowsing off, she wondered, or was the experience of meeting that person in her "highest and best good" after all? Maybe it was some kind of life lesson, or maybe it helped her clarify what she wanted in a relationship. As discussed previously, dowsing about future events (divination) presents some challenges.

Love is one area where dowsing can provide some—but, of course, not all—of the answers. You can ask if someone would potentially be a good partner for you, if someone is honest and trustworthy, if he or she is capable of unconditional love or interested in a lasting relationship. Try asking, "How compatible are we?" using the counting method or the percentage chart (figure 3-6).

Greg Nielsen in *Beyond Pendulum Power* suggests ranking a relationship in five areas of compatibility: spiritual, mental, energy, emotional, and physical. By energy, he means whether a couple feels energized by being together, drained, or somewhere in between. Do a pendulum reading ranking each area on a one-to-ten scale. Then add up the scores and multiply by two. A score of 90 to 100 is superior and 75 to 89 is excellent.[1]

One caveat, though. If seeking a lasting relationship is at the top of your list of priorities, you may find it difficult to dowse accurately about love. I know that was certainly true for me. Emotional attachments to an issue can cloud our dowsing, acting like a "filter" that skews results. If you know that is true for you, be extraordinarily careful in your preparations. Center yourself and get into the proper, detached state. Ask your ego, and all of its needs and wants, to step aside. Be sure to ask whether this is something you can explore with dowsing. Check to see whether there are any blocks that would keep you from getting clear answers and, if so, remove them. You may even want to preface your questions with the declaration, "Tell me the truth!" Blind dowsing, as discussed in chapter three, may also be helpful when asking about prospective relationships.

Although dowsing can be problematic in potential relationships, it can be extremely valuable in existing relationships, where understanding what is happening beneath the surface can help smooth tensions with your partner, friends, or family members. If we are in a relationship with someone and want to use our intuition to improve that relationship, I believe that is a perfectly acceptable use of our dowsing skills. To be sure, always ask permission before you start.

You might want to prepare for this type of intuitive session by doing a short meditation. Hold as your intention that you want to heal a particular, specific problem in your relationship, for example. Your goal is to understand the needs and motivations of the person you are involved with. I suggest that you begin by asking questions to help pinpoint what you feel might be going wrong. Ask your subconscious self, "What incident has disturbed me recently in this relationship?" You may think of several; if so, check with your pendulum to see which relates the most to the problem at hand. Then ask yourself, "When that incident happened, what feelings did it trigger in me?" Refer to the list of underlying emotional states (figure 5-1) and dowse to see which you get a hit on: anger, sad, confused, hurt, stunned, lonely, and so on. This can give you more clarity about your reaction to the situation.

Now, shift your focus to connect to universal consciousness. Concentrate on your partner and ask, "What did he (or she) want from me when this incident occurred?" Go through as many things as you can think of: tenderness, love, control, power, appreciation, attention, to gain the upper hand, to win, to hurt me. Then ask, "What does he need from me?" and "How will he react when he gets what he needs?" *Want* and *need* are two very different things. A person may want to control a situation, but what he or she may need is to feel powerful.

See what conclusions you can draw about your situation. For instance, Kim wanted to gain clarity about an argument she had with her husband, who was very stressed. On reflecting about the incident, she felt that "he wants me to be as stressed as he is," but she learned that what he really needs is to feel more secure. When that need is met, he would be able to relax. Thanks to this exercise, Kim resolved not to react to her husband when he was stressed out, but instead to offer ways to help him relax. A backrub and hot bath would be a better strategy than snapping back at him. This relationship exercise was inspired by the Buddhist practice of Chöd, as described by Tsultrim Allione in *Feeding Your Demons*.[2]

There are many questions we wonder about in our relationships: Is my wife satisfied with our lovemaking? Is my son having difficulty with friends at school? Is there something that I can do to make life easier for my sister? Have I angered my mother? Is it best to apologize or let it be? As long as our intention is to better our relationships, dowsing can be a wonderful tool to help resolve issues with our family and friends.

9

Dowsing for Companion Animals

If you could talk to animals like Dr. Doolittle, imagine what you could discover. Are there health problems with your pet that a vet hasn't been able to solve? Do you ever wonder what is going on emotionally with your animal that is causing behavioral issues in your home? Many people, including a fair number of "curious skeptics," have hired animal communicators to get answers to these kinds of questions. With dowsing, you can learn to be your own animal communicator and gather valuable information that can help you and your pet.

Bill Northern, an animal communicator in Warsaw, Virginia, believes dowsing can provide a clear, accurate means of connecting with animals. He specializes in dowsing health problems for horses. Northern started dowsing in 1994, when a plumbing emergency had him searching for the sewer line for his paper supply business. Someone from city government came over first with the engineering plans, then an electronic sounding device, and finally, when the digging was still unsuccessful, dowsing rods. "Sure enough, the dowsing rods found what we were looking for. And I got them in my hands, and they worked for me," said Northern.

That summer, he traveled to Vermont to attend the annual convention of the American Society of Dowsers. One of the presenters brought in two horses and gave the students in her class twenty questions to dowse, such as, "Does this horse like children?" "Does this horse like to jump?" and "Does this horse have a clubbed foot?" Northern, although he had been around horses all his life, didn't do very well, getting seven or eight correct out of twenty. "But there were people there from New York City that hardly would know a horse from a cow, and they were getting seventeen and eighteen right."

"It came to me right then that, if I could learn to do this, I could save people an awful lot of money on vet bills," he said. That is exactly what he does now, working for horse owners and trainers from Panama, France, Ireland, Sweden, Hawaii, New Zealand (where he winters) and Kentucky (where he spends each spring). Most of his work is done remotely. He can sit in his chair in Virginia and connect with an animal virtually anywhere.

Northern only handles one remote call a day because it is so taxing. About fifteen minutes before each appointment, he centers himself and meditates. "I don't answer the telephone. I don't do anything but just try to clear everything out of my head, so I can listen." He only needs the name of the animal, an address, and the name of the person that the animal is connected to.

That surprises some people who think you need to be next to the animal you are dowsing. However, the theory of nonlocal awareness, as discussed in chapter two, can help explain why that's not necessary. That principle explains that we are all interconnected, and our consciousness is not hindered by issues of space or time. We can be aware of something happening far away from us because everything is connected. In other words, quantum interconnectedness allows us to dowse accurately whether the subject we are working with is next to us or halfway around the world.

Usually, Northern uses a model of a horse and his pendulum to focus on the animal and zero in on areas of concern. "If it's a hot nail in a horse's hoof, we can pinpoint it. Quite often, we'll pinpoint an abscess within a half-inch of where it is," he said. "The more you do this, the easier it gets. The more you do it, the more precise you are."

If Northern is any indication, dowsing can also cause your intuitive gifts to grow. About four years after he started dowsing horses, he began to "hear" horses, too. His clairaudient sensitivity allows him to "hear" in his head what a horse is thinking. He also does remote viewing, which he says enables him to look through a horse's eyes, or enter a horse's body and look at its organs. "What I'll do is first ask this horse if he thinks he has any ulcers or that he might have a problem with his stomach. And if he says no, then I don't bother. But if he says yes, my stomach hurts a lot, then I will just go in and have a look and see what I see."

Northern has worked for some of the big horse farms in Kentucky when there are health issues with a horse that a vet can't solve or when other questions arise. Recently a leading breeder in France called him the day before the sale of a million-dollar thoroughbred. The breeder wanted to know whether the horse had the right temperament for racing. Before making a seven-figure investment, he asked Northern to dowse the horse for him.

Northern thinks dowsing is a particularly good way to connect to animals. "Most people who learn animal communication learn it through meditation," he said. But meditation can sometimes allow other animals to come through, "who aren't who you want to listen to ... With dowsing with your pendulum, you stay more focused."

Northern warned it may be difficult to dowse your own animal if you are too emotionally attached, just as with other sensitive topics. The rational brain kicks in and tries to find the answer, which may negatively affect your dowsing results. As discussed previously, center yourself and remove any blocks that may be present before attempting to dowse your own pet.

There doesn't have to be a major health issue going on with your animal to try dowsing. You can check in about any number of things, either physical or emotional. For instance, Brigid was having a behavioral problem with Max, a shelter cat that had refused to use his litter box for more than a year. Brigid tried moving the litter box several times in an attempt to find a place that Max would like better. She changed the cat litter to a clay-based version that was potentially more appealing to indoor-outdoor cats because it feels more like dirt. Nothing worked. Max avoided the box and took care of matters in the back yard.

That was fine while the family was home, but they were getting ready to head to the Pacific Northwest for the holidays. Was it safe to leave Max at home with just a cat sitter to check on him? A trip to Cape Cod six months earlier had been a disaster. Max had accidents all over the house. "I was very nervous about leaving him," Brigid said.

She asked me to dowse the situation and see what I could find. First, I asked whether the issue was mainly physical or mainly emotional. I got a positive swing on it being an emotional issue. I referred to the list of underlying emotional states (figure 5-1) and asked what Max was feeling when the family went out of town. "Fear" and "nervousness" got positive responses. Then I started asking questions related to the situation: "Is there a better place for the litter box? Is it in the basement, on the first floor, or upstairs?" I narrowed the location to the upstairs and then started asking about specific rooms. I told Brigid that the best location for the litter box was in the large kids' bathroom in the center of the upper floor. I also suggested that she keep a radio on while they were away, so that it would sound like there was more activity in the house.

Brigid called me three days later to say that Max had used the litter box over the weekend. Amazed and encouraged, she felt better about leaving her persnickety cat for the holidays.

The information Brigid got from our session helped her set up the situation for success. First, she moved the litter box to a more emotionally comfortable place for her cat and got him in the habit of using it before she left. She arranged for a neighborhood girl to check on Max twice a day. The eleven-year-old played with and stroked Max, giving him reassurance and helping ease a difficult time for him. And by chance, Brigid's son left his alarm on over the vacation, so the radio blared for an hour each morning, which sounded as if there were people in the house. Brigid was thrilled when she returned home to a happy cat and a well-used litter box. "I never, ever would have thought to put the litter box upstairs," she said. Luckily, dowsing prompts us to ask the right questions.

DOWSING FOR ANIMAL HEALTH ISSUES

If you'd like to try to intuitively connect to your pet or another animal, first center yourself, taking several deep breaths. Ask whether it's okay to dowse about this animal at this time. If it is your own pet, ask to remove any unconscious blocks that would keep your dowsing from being completely accurate.

Figure 9-1, the animal health chart, will allow you to gather more information about any problem the pet may be having. Using your pendulum, first determine

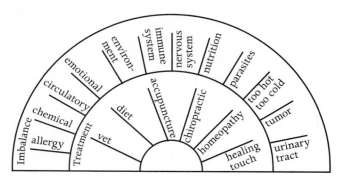

Figure 9-1: Animal health chart

whether the problem is physical or emotional. If you get a mixed response, you can check the proportion of each (physical versus emotional) using the one-to-ten counting method or the percentage chart (figure 3-6). Whether the problem is physical or emotional in nature, the next ring on the chart can tell you which treatment would be best, and the outer ring can help pinpoint the cause. Ask the question, "What do I need to pay attention to? Show me areas of disturbance." If "nutrition" gets a hit, for example, look into the animal's diet. You can also dowse the list of underlying emotional states (figure 5-1) for more insight.

If you know there is a behavioral issue, try to come up with questions that are specific to that problem, as

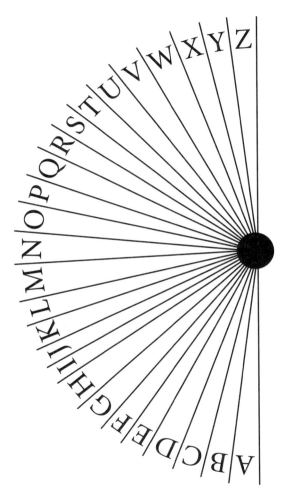

Figure 9-2: ABC chart

we did with Brigid's cat. Is the house too cold for this animal? Is she bothered by my other cat? Is this horse ready to retire? Would my dogs be happier in another location?

Another tool you may find useful is the ABC chart (figure 9-2), which allows you to communicate directly with your pet. To do this, center yourself and ask to connect only to this animal and no one else. Then ask your pet, "What do you want to tell me?" Hold your pendulum over the chart and see if it points to any letters. Try not to engage your logical brain to guess what word is being spelled out. Some people are more skilled at this technique than others, but you can learn to do it with practice. The two key points are to make sure you are connecting to the right animal, and to make sure your brain is not getting in the way. (You can also use this technique to communicate with a deceased loved one, as briefly mentioned in chapter four. Remember to close the connection when you are finished.)

This method can be helpful if you need clarification about what your pet wants. "More food" was the answer from one aging cat—more specifically, eggs. This resonated for the cat's owner, because whenever she and her husband ate soft-boiled eggs, the cat waited eagerly to lick the inside of the shells. Another cat owner was able to determine that her pet was cold and might benefit from sleeping on a heated pad. It was a simple fix that was greeted with purring contentment. Who knows what else our pets can tell us, if only we ask?

❧ 10 ❧

Instant Intuition
for Your Career

Business success comes down to making good decisions, which often have to be done very quickly.
You might not have the luxury of doing a complete
analysis of a situation before acting. You might have
incomplete or conflicting information, or the situation
might be changing rapidly. That's when many business
leaders would agree they have to rely on their intuition
to come up with the right answers.

Research shows that the most effective leaders rely
on their gut instincts to help run their businesses. A
study at the New Jersey Institute of Technology found
that 80 percent of executives whose companies experienced profits that doubled over a five-year period were
shown to have above average powers of intuition.[1]

Some people think that intuition is really our ability to recognize patterns that are similar to past experiences. We may not remember the details, but somehow we can process the similarities instantly and come up with an "aha moment" that is actually a message from our subconscious mind in the form of a gut feeling. Dowsing allows us to communicate with the subconscious at will, and as often as needed. Using the techniques described in this book, you can apply "intuition in an instant" to any pressing business issue that comes across your desk. Whether it is making a split-second decision or pondering a larger question in your career like a job change, using your inner wisdom can be invaluable. Karen was working in Europe, and was looking for a job that would either take her to a different foreign country or back home to the United States. Aidan was about to uproot his entire family and move several hundred miles away for a job he was uncertain was right for him. Margaret was frustrated in a high-powered job with a hotel chain, where she was being micromanaged by her boss. And Josh needed to prepare for a difficult meeting with his partner in which they would negotiate the terms of splitting their business. In each of these critical situations, dowsing provided clear answers and helped the people involved make the right decision for themselves.

Instead of using simple yes-or-no questions, we were able to get more depth and clarity using the one-to-ten counting method, as discussed in chapter three. It's a technique that can be used for many different purposes and lends itself well to the area of business.

To try it, hold your pendulum and keep your question in mind as you count slowly in your head from one to ten. You will get a spin on the number that applies to your question. It can help to think in terms of percentages. Five and under are low scores. Six and seven are average. Eight and nine are strong, and ten is the strongest and most positive response. An eight, or 80 percent, is good, but not as positive as a nine (90 percent) or a ten (100 percent).

A handy way to use this method is to prioritize your day's work. Write out your to-do list for the day and dowse each item, asking to be shown its relative priority. In other words, you will rank each item in order of importance. It's interesting to note that some tasks you thought were most important to accomplish on a given day get moved to the bottom of your list.

You can also use this technique to rank ideas you have for new projects. Should you focus your efforts in the next few months on writing, teaching, looking for a new job, or targeting new sales from a certain demographic? I like to brainstorm all my ideas for new projects on a large drawing pad. It gives me room to create a flow chart if I need it, or to diagram or draw circles around certain topics. Try putting each major idea on a different part of the paper. Then you can actually map-dowse the paper while holding the question in your mind, "Where should I focus my attention at this time?" Once you get a positive response, you can go through all the subtopics under that heading and dowse them on the one-to-ten scale. For example, if "teaching" gets the most positive spin for you, you can then ask about teaching at the community college, offering small classes in your home, doing online webinars, and so on, and rank the possibilities with the intention of pursuing the most promising ideas first.

CASE I: LOOKING FOR WORK

Karen loved living and working in Europe. A job had brought her to Prague years before, but it wasn't the work that was the biggest draw. It was the opportunity to travel easily to so many world-class cities. Berlin, Paris, and Amsterdam were regular weekend jaunts. But a change in management made her work situation difficult. She simply did not want to work for her new boss, so she started looking for a different job—literally, anywhere in the world.

When we first looked at her situation with the pendulum, we got a positive swing for the question, "Is the time right for Karen to make a change in her work?" Then we used a calendar to see when the timing would be best for applying for work. Similar to the one-to-ten method, I named the months of the year while I held the pendulum. November and December got positive swings, so I encouraged her to increase her job-hunting efforts during those months. Then we looked at when a move might be likely. April got a positive swing. Even though questions regarding the future are tricky and can be affected by many variables, we decided to ask anyway.

Because she was looking at many different industries, we ranked each to show her where she might concentrate her efforts. Her dream job would be a position in human resources at Google, or at a company she admired that manufactured children's toys. News and information companies ranked a ten, followed by technology firms (six), government agencies (five), and children's toy companies (four).

After conducting a major job search and applying for human resources jobs in various fields, Karen was interviewed by a major news organization based in New York City in December of that year. They offered her the job in February and she moved back to the United States in April, just as the pendulum had predicted.

CASE 2: EVALUATING A JOB OFFER

Aidan was so miserable in his current position that he jumped at the first job offer he received, even though it was a lateral move. He would receive the same salary and have roughly the same responsibilities. However, he would need to move his family to a more expensive area of the country. Nancy, Aidan's wife, was supportive but concerned about the implications of the move. Together, we evaluated the various factors involved in the decision using the one-to-ten ranking system.

Overall, Aidan's new job ranked a five, a pretty mediocre score. But we wanted to look at all of its particulars, so we asked about the challenge of the work itself (three); his boss and coworkers (nine); the stability of the job (eight); Aidan's commute, which would be longer (five); quality of life in this new location (seven); the potential for Nancy to find freelance work (four); housing (four); and the effect on their financial situation if they made the move (three).

The next day, Aidan called his new boss and told her that he had changed his mind. Looking closely at each factor, and assigning a ranking to it, allowed Aidan to step back and assess the situation more neutrally. Nothing that we discovered working with the pendulum was a surprise to him. In his heart, he knew all along what was the right decision. Dowsing just provided more proof.

CASE 3: WORKING WITH PEOPLE

Margaret was working at her dream job, but she wasn't working for her dream boss. She felt like he was looking over her shoulder at all times, constantly evaluating her performance. Margaret wanted to explore whether she had reasons to feel paranoid at work. We began by asking a series of yes-or-no questions: Was there a problem between her and her boss? Did he approve of the work she was doing? Was there a way to improve her work situation? Was it a matter of her documenting the work she was already doing? Each of these questions got a positive response, but the last was an enormously strong swing. I then did a one-to-ten ranking to find out how important this issue was to her job security. It was a ten. Based on that information, I told Margaret that I felt she needed to protect herself by documenting all the work she was doing in e-mails and memos. This seemed reasonable to her.

When Margaret returned to work after a short vacation, she was able to look at her job with a different perspective. She recognized that her boss was extremely dependent on his BlackBerry, and that the corporate culture in the hotel chain revolved around nearly constant BlackBerry updates. Since she wasn't comfortable with that technology, Margaret realized she would be happier if she made a job change. She switched jobs shortly afterward and is extremely satisfied in her new position.

CASE 4: NEGOTIATING

Josh was a partner in a company whose business was beginning to falter. Although he resisted believing it, his partner had mismanaged the company's affairs and may have even pilfered its accounts. Josh wanted to be able to maintain some of his clients and, most importantly, get out of the noncompete clause that he had signed. He was not confident that he would be able to negotiate even that, let alone walk away from the deal with some cash in hand.

We started by first asking the question, "Does Josh need a lawyer to advise him before the meeting?" The answer was a strong yes. Then we dowsed for which lawyer would be best, since Josh worked with several. Next we looked at the calendar to pinpoint which day would be best for Josh to travel to New York to negotiate with his partner. Holding the pendulum over each day in the calendar, I identified the second week in September as an ideal time for a meeting. Then we asked a series of questions: Is it in Josh's best interest to completely sever his business relationship with his partner? Will Josh get out of his noncompete clause? Will Josh maintain some of his clients? Will he walk away with some cash? All the questions were answered positively.

Josh walked into the meeting in a positive frame of mind and, with the help of his lawyer, was able to negotiate exactly what he wanted. He walked away with several major clients, along with some cash, easing the transition to working on his own. Most importantly, after a year's wait, his noncompete clause will be null and void.

Using intuition in business has countless applications. It can provide a trusted second opinion on the important decisions that need to be made. A school psychologist I know dowses when evaluating the students assigned to her. A reading teacher dowses to determine which approach is best for her students. A literary agent uses her pendulum to decide which clients to sign. An actress chooses between two roles she is offered that will be staged at the same time. Each of these people could make these decisions without any intuitive guidance, but they feel more secure in their decisions when using the pendulum.

According to a study done by the American Society of Dowsers, a majority of the people who responded dowse on the job. That is no surprise, since dowsing can provide instant access to our intuitive minds and help with critical decision making. We all want to feel confident in the decisions we make and the course we set for ourselves. Becoming skilled in asking business questions, both logically and intuitively, can give us a competitive edge.

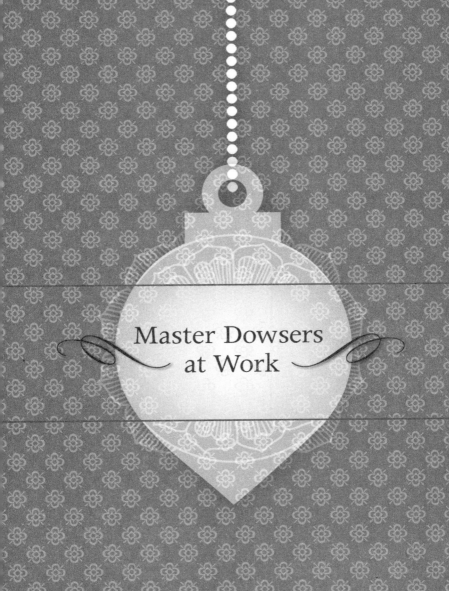

Master Dowsers
at Work

∽ 11 ∾

Finding Water and More

Finding water is perhaps the oldest and best-known use for the intuitive technique that you've learned to apply to personal health and wellness, relationships, and business. Water dowsing is a valuable skill, especially in areas of the country without public drinking water. A good master dowser is in high demand, since the cost of drilling a well runs in the thousands of dollars. No one wants to drill a dry hole.

John Wayne Blassingame didn't start off dowsing for water. He was looking for pipes—hundreds of feet of irrigation pipes buried somewhere in the desert on the grounds of a munitions depot in Hawthorne, Nevada. As part of a Navy training exercise with a construction battalion, Blassingame, a new chief petty officer, was assigned a crew of men to find the buried pipe. The Marines were planning a nine-hole golf course and needed an irrigation system for sprinklers. The problem was that no one knew exactly where the pipe was hidden.

Blassingame had his crew of more than thirty men working in the blazing sun for days, with three or four backhoes digging holes all over the desert. "If you could have seen it from the air, it would have looked like a bunch of moles," he said, laughing. They didn't turn up much more than a rattlesnake or two. Finally, an old Navy officer came up to Blassingame and told him he was making a fool of himself in front of his men. The man asked him for a pair of metal rods so he could do some "witching." Blassingame watched as the officer bent the rods and took off across the desert. "He only walked about a hundred yards and he says, 'Just come over and dig right here.' Just like that, he found the pipe. And it was deep, five feet deep. So I said, 'Give me those damn things. Let me see if I can do that.' So I walked across there and, sure enough, I had the same sensitivity that he did."

That was on a Wednesday after they had been digging for two days. "Before noon, we had found every one of those pipes," he said.

That was how John Wayne Blassingame started dowsing. By the mid-1970s, he was doing it professionally, dowsing wells in five or six counties in California. Finding water in that state can be tricky, he said. "It's like a bowl of jelly because of the earthquakes." The faults in the earth can cause water to shift after a quake. Wells need to be deeper, and sealed to fifty feet, as opposed to areas of the country where "dug wells" are allowed.

Blassingame, now in his eighties, lives in Lyndonville, Vermont, with his wife and daughter. Dowsing keeps him young, he claims, and dowsing a well energizes him. He has his own unique way of working. First he fills out a sheet that he's devised called "Dowsing Parameters." Your subconscious mind needs to know exactly what you want to find, Blassingame explained. "If you just go out and say, 'I'm looking for water,' you're likely to find a garbage dump or something, so you have to be very specific about what you're looking for. And then you won't find anything else."

The sheet begins, "While dowsing for this well site, I will have asked my dowsing system the 'May I, Can I, Should I' questions and made sure that all influences from earth energies or deposits, thoughts, imaging, wishes, desires, or biases from any source, physical or nonphysical, including my own and/or other persons, entities, or mind systems of any kind, affect me or my dowsing answers only in a positive manner."

After that, the sheet spells out exactly what he wants to find. For example, he is trying to pinpoint a legal domestic well site, a primary water source, water that is potable and palatable, water that has a pH factor of 6 to 8, water that will flow all year, that has a temperature of 90 degrees or less, that flows at a minimum of five gallons per minute recoverable at the surface, at a safe, practical, and cost-effective location for the property owner and driller, and with a depth search for veins or water sources to be less than five hundred feet.

Blassingame goes over his dowsing parameters every time. "I read it to customers, so they know exactly what I'm looking for." When he gets to the site, he straps on a leather tool belt outfitted with metal L-rods, plastic Y-rods, a bobber, surveying flags, and other tools that help him dowse on site. Then, out of the back of his truck, he pulls out a long rod he designed to help ground him and connect to the earth's energy. This "Texas T-rod" is made of 3/8-inch case-hardened steel welded into a T-shape so that the short end is a handle he can hold on to. The proportions are exactly 1:1.618, the "golden mean" of sacred geometry, or *phi*. He bangs that big T-rod into the ground, holds on to it with his left hand, and holds a smaller L-rod in his right hand. Slowly, he turns in a circle, asking himself, "Where is the water?" When his L-rod crosses to his chest, it means his left hand on the

T-rod is pointed at the water vein. "Thank you, thank you, thank you," he says, cultivating what he calls "an attitude of gratitude."

Now he "triangulates" the site, leaving the T-rod pointing in the direction of the vein. He pulls his two brass L-rods out of his belt and walks in a straight line from the T-rod. When his rods cross, he marks a spot in the grass with a stake. That is the outer edge of the water vein. He double-checks that spot from various angles.

Then he holds one L-rod loosely in the air as a pointer and asks, "Which way should I walk to find the other edge of this energy?" When he locates the other edge of the water system, he marks it. Finally, he works inside those boundaries, saying, "Show me where in between is the best spot for a well. Is this the best spot?" When he gets his "yes," he marks it and continues to check it from different angles—tweaking it, he says.

Once Blassingame is confident that he has found the right spot to site the well, he puts away his L-rod and pulls a blue plastic Y-rod out of his tool belt. He holds it at arm's length with the end pointed up toward the bill of his Navy baseball cap. Again, he begins a dialogue. "I need info about this water. Can I get it to the surface? Yes." The Y-rod pulls down toward the ground with some force. He swings it up into position again.

"Will it bring up more than five gallons a minute? Yes. More than ten? Yes. More than twelve?" Using this process, he determines that the well site will meet all his parameters for good, potable drinking water and come in at about eleven or twelve gallons per minute, with a maximum depth of 250 feet.

With what he estimates at more than a thousand well sites under his belt, Blassingame is one of the most experienced water dowsers in the northeast. But he is not the only one. Bruce Irwin, the master dowser in New York, is another.

Irwin has dowsed hundreds of wells from Pennsylvania to Canada. One of the biggest he ever worked on was the entire water supply for the town of Petersburg in upstate New York. Not only did he manage to site three wells drawing sufficient water to meet the needs of six hundred families, but he located the wells uphill so that they gravity-feed down to the pumping station, saving the town substantial electricity charges on a year-round basis.

Edith Greene, an eighty-year-old Vermont dowser, was the savior of the town of Montgomery, whose municipal wells were pumping arsenic-laced water in 1999. Literally, the water was poison. The town leaders spent hundreds of thousands of dollars drilling for a new well and were at the point of desperation when they called on Greene to help them. She was able to locate a well pumping three hundred gallons a minute, three times what Montgomery needed.

But the numbers of people who specialize in water dowsing are few, compared to those who dowse for information, or other specialties. As the survey from the American Society of Dowsers showed, only 38 percent of the respondents dowse for water, versus 81 percent who dowse for information.

Arvid Johnson, operations manager for the American Society of Dowsers, thinks this is because so much is at stake. "You go out and drill a water well, they're gonna drill. And they're gonna get paid whatever it is, twenty-five dollars a foot. It can run into a couple thousand dollars pretty quickly, and if you are wrong ... I think that water dowsers are rarer because there are fewer people willing to put so much on the line for water dowsing."

Unless someone lives in a rural area where wells are the norm, the need isn't there, either. Why would someone who lived in an urban or suburban environment need to dowse for water when they could simply turn on a tap? At this point, you may be asking yourself the same question: why do I need to know how to find water? Quite frankly, you don't. But dowsing for water is dowsing at its most elemental. It is how it began, perhaps back in prehistoric times. Finding water with our intuitive skills alone is our birthright, and yet so few of us know how to do it.

Greg Storozuk, a former president of the American Society of Dowsers, thinks there's a good reason that we should learn. At the 2008 ASD convention, he challenged the audience to go out in their back yards or a local park and find a vein of underground drinking water less than a foot deep. Dig down until you see a trickle of water to confirm that your dowsing is on target. Hone this basic skill, he advised, because the ability to find water is essential to us as human beings, and may be needed at some point for survival. "We're living in an age of terrorism. Suppose somebody decides to take out the grid. Then what?" he asked.[1]

While that may seem alarmist to some, there is no denying the need for water worldwide is a growing problem. The United Nations has reported that 1.1 billion people across the globe don't have access to safe drinking water.[2] With water a dwindling resource in many parts of the world, dowsing can once again be an essential life skill, just as it was for our early ancestors. Steve Herbert runs Water for Humanity, an organization whose purpose is to fund water resources development worldwide and demonstrate the practical applications of dowsing. Each year, Water for Humanity sends grants to fund wells in places like Haiti, Honduras, India, and Africa. Working with an all-volunteer staff and a budget of approximately $25,000 per year (mostly donations from American Society of Dowsers members), the organization pays for a dozen or more water projects, like drilled and dug wells, pumps, rainwater harvesting, water purification, and composting latrines. During the winter when he has more free time, Herbert travels to a location and trains dowsers, a process that he says is empowering to the rural farmers he often works with. "It's much more productive to go and teach people to dowse and they teach other people to dowse. So it snowballs and creates many more dowsers than just a few trying to do all the work."

Sometimes, all it takes is a quick demonstration for a person to discover his or her own natural dowsing ability. On a trip to coastal Ecuador, an arid place in the rain shadow of the Andes, Herbert gave a brief introduction to dowsing. The following year he returned to present a more formal training session. One woman in his class told him that she had hired a man who had seen Herbert's demonstration the year before, and he successfully found water on her challenging property. "The drill couldn't even penetrate the rock, it was so hard," said Herbert. "So this guy had not only to dowse for where to find water, he had to dowse for where the rock was soft enough to penetrate to get at it."

DOWSING FOR A WATER VEIN

If you want to try dowsing for water, go out in your back yard, or in a local park, with your dowsing tools. Most people who dowse in the field use a pair of L-rods. They are steadier to use outside, where the wind might blow around a pendulum. But take your pendulum, too, or a Y-rod or bobber, for the secondary questions you will ask.

Center yourself and ask permission to dowse for water in this area. Then think about what you are looking for. If you want to site a well for home use, you might keep in mind the parameters that Bruce Irwin uses. He looks for drinking water that is potable, without sulfur, iron, or other contaminants that would make it undesirable. The water will draw at least five gallons per minute and be found at a depth of less than three hundred feet. Finally, no one else will depend on that water vein for drinking water.

But if you are dowsing for water just as an exercise for yourself, you might want to follow Greg Storozuk's plan and dowse for a shallow water vein that will satisfy this requirement: a vein of free-flowing water that can be found less than twelve inches underground. See if you can hold an image of that target in your mind. Hold your L-rods parallel to the ground and double-check your positive response by asking, "Show me a yes." Your rods will either cross or open wide. Then ask, "Show me an indication when I am facing the target." Turn slowly in a circle and watch for your rods to move. When you get a reaction from your rods, stop. If you are in a small area like a back yard, you can just start walking in that direction, asking your rods, "Show me when I am on the edge of this water vein." But if you have a bigger area to cover, you might ask, "How many paces am I from the nearest edge of this water vein? Five? Ten? Twenty?" If you get a positive hit on twenty, double-check whether it is under or over twenty-five paces until you pinpoint the correct number. Then start walking while counting your steps. See if your rods cross when you've walked that many paces. When you get an indication you are on the edge of the water vein, mark the spot with a flag or another identifier. Now find the other edge of the water vein by repeating the same steps. Finally, ask, "Show me an indication when I am on the best spot to dig for water less than twelve inches deep." When you get a positive reaction from your rods, mark the spot.

At this point when dowsing a well site, professional dowsers often switch to a Y-rod, bobber, or pendulum to ask specific questions about the site, such as how deep the water vein is and how many gallons a minute it will draw. Often, they will double-check that the site meets all the conditions that they were hoping to find—that the water is good and clean, without contaminants, for instance, and that no one else is relying on it for their water supply.

Now that you've marked the best spot to find water less than a foot deep, your work is almost done. All that is left is to start digging.

EASY STEPS FOR DOWSING FOR WATER LESS THAN A FOOT DEEP

- Center yourself and ask whether you can dowse in this area.
- Ask to find a vein of water less than twelve inches underground.
- Holding your L-rods, slowly turn in a circle and ask for an indication when you are facing the target. Stop when you get a response.
- Start walking in that direction and ask for an indication when you are on the edge of the water vein. Mark the spot.
- Repeat the process to find the other edge of the water vein.

- Now, with both edges marked, walk between them and ask for the best spot to dig for water less than twelve inches deep. Mark the spot and dig to see whether your dowsing was correct.

WHAT ELSE LIES BENEATH?

Water is just the start of what can be found underground with dowsing: pipes, property markers, buried coins, gold and other treasure, even oil.

But it was tunnels that captured the imagination of Louis Matacia, a professional land surveyor working as a consultant to the Marines in November 1966. America was at war in Vietnam, and Matacia had just watched a film depicting U.S. troops struggling to locate enemy tunnels in the thick jungle terrain. In the film, Robert McNamara, the U.S. Secretary of Defense, asked for innovative ideas to help solve some of the military's toughest problems. Matacia figured dowsing might be able to help.

Not surprisingly, his initial dowsing demonstration was met with a fair amount of skepticism. But his boss at Quantico told him to head to a mock Vietcong village on the base that the Marines used as a tactical training site. Matacia got to work and almost immediately had success in finding tunnels, underground communication wires, pipes, and hidden rooms behind false walls.

"I found everything in fifteen minutes that it took them years to put together," he said.

Excited by the prospect that dowsing could save soldiers' lives in the field, Matacia sent letters to a dozen Defense Department research agencies about the potential uses of dowsing in military operations. When they all turned him down, he shot a home movie with no sound showing close-ups of Marines using dowsing rods to locate targets. He passed the film to a friend, a colonel who was headed to Vietnam. "I said, 'Would you take this down to the Marines and see if they can make it work for them?'"

Apparently, it did. By October 1966, The *New York Times*' Hanson Baldwin reported, "Coat-hanger dowsers, as they are called here, are not included in Marine Corps equipment manuals. But, according to Marine officers, they have been used in Vietnam with marked success in the last year, particularly by engineer units of the First and Third Marine Divisions, which are engaged in mine detection and tunnel destruction."[3]

Matacia's film was doing in Vietnam what he had not received permission to do himself: teach Marines to dowse. "In other words, I did it without anybody's authority. So I sent it over there and consequently they used it and it was very successful for them. And they found things that I never knew were there," like a Vietcong mailing system using buried bamboo tubes.

Ultimately, military officials deemed dowsing too unscientific to be officially included in military training. But Matacia still thinks dowsing can save the lives of soldiers in combat. A CD copy of his military handbook has a handwritten invitation at the top: "Make a copy for yourself and send a copy to a soldier."[4]

These days, the eighty-year-old Virginian still works as a land surveyor in four states, and in his free time hunts for treasure. It's a difficult dowsing task, and just as dangerous as being in a war zone. "Treasure hunting is just like combat," he said. Some Civil War treasure is mined with explosives, he said, and people are watching you all the time. Safer, although bone-wearying, is digging thirty inches down in wet sand for buried trinkets on Virginia Beach. To avoid attention, Matacia and a team of three others work at night in wet suits, one serving as the locator, two as diggers, and one as the retriever. They can gather a bucketful of jewelry and coins on a good night, he said.

Some dowsers use special compartments on their dowsing rods to hold a bit of the object they are seeking, like gold, for instance. Treasure dowsing techniques are closely guarded secrets, as they are in dowsing for oil, or doodle-bugging as it's sometimes called. But Matacia was willing to share some tips. The most important one, he said, is to ask the question, "Can this treasure be recovered by me?" If not, he recommends abandoning the target.

Matacia also warned treasure hunters to watch for entrapment; don't tell anyone what you are looking for. Don't trespass. Be sure to check out property ownership records in the county courthouse. Observe the rules wherever you are, whether on U.S. or state park land, Bureau of Land Management property, military installations, or Indian reservations. Also, he said, be aware of regulations regarding Native American artifacts in offshore areas, which are protected by strict government policies. Finally, you can't just be an "armchair explorer." "You got to work at this stuff in the field," he said. "Go dig some holes and bring things back."

Matacia dowses for other kinds of treasure as well: he located six successful oil wells and is working on a natural gas project in southwest Virginia. The company that leases the land brought in an instrument to tell them how thick the shale was on the site Matacia selected, and it registered as the biggest find they ever had. In this case, Matacia's map dowsing was an example of "armchair" treasure hunting that paid off.

∾ 12 ∾

Dowsing in the Home

Your intuitive skills can be used to explore the environment inside your home, as well as outside. Just as you learned to detect the energy pattern of a water vein underground, you can check for harmful energies in your living areas that might impact your health.

Aches, pains, and general malaise are bringing Leroy Bull a lot of business these days. The master dowser in Doylestown, Pennsylvania, revealed that 60 percent of his business is helping people discover what about their homes is making them sick. Referrals come from word of mouth and from the health food store, where his business card is handed out to people who are trying to figure out why they feel so lousy. Typically, people will call after they move to a new house and tell him,

"It's all been downhill since." They've been to dozens of doctors, who all say there's nothing wrong with them.

Many dowsers believe that underground water veins flowing under a house have the potential to negatively affect the people living there, especially if the veins cross or come together under a place where a person spends a lot of time, like a bedroom, for instance. Natural radiation can rise up through the earth at areas of stress, affected by underground water, faults and cavities in the ground, and other factors. A home also can be negatively affected by electromagnetic fields given off inside by appliances, lighting, and wiring, and outside from transformers and electrical power lines.

In the 1970s, an Austrian study done by Käthe Bachler looked at three thousand apartments in fourteen countries. Among her findings, a sample of five hundred cancer cases showed that all the patients were sleeping over areas of geopathic stress, and 95 percent of children with health and behavioral problems slept or worked at desks over places that gave off these kinds of harmful rays.[1]

People who are sensitive to these energies can feel them acutely. When Edith Greene, the Vermont master dowser, enters a home afflicted with them, she feels like she's hit a wall. "Oh, it makes you feel like you have a bad cold," she says. That's why she makes sure she protects herself before heading out on a dowsing job, imagining a circle of protection all the way around her. If she doesn't, she can feel dizzy and ill after doing a clearing.

Bull tells his clients what they can do to fix some of the problems. Instead of expensive electronic interference machines, he often suggests stringing a piece of sixteen-gauge wire around the base of a house. The ends should come together in a completed circuit like the letter O, without being tied off. There are other inexpensive ways to fix some problems, such as dropping magnets outside at the base of a transformer, for example. Bull often works with his wife, Diane, who is a dowser and feng shui consultant. "Very often, for example, we'll get a big house and I'll do the dowsing on the outside and she'll do feng shui on the inside. We can get a lot done in a day that way." She dowses to see what feng shui "cures" are needed, and then she dowses afterward to see whether they've worked.

Eileen Weklar is a feng shui consultant in Arlington, Virginia who also uses dowsing in her work. In fact, she was taught to dowse by her first feng shui teacher. Dowsing is similar to feng shui, she says, because both practices are seeking answers through energy.

Weklar dowses before she even arrives at a client's home to see if there is any information she needs to bring on a topic that wasn't discussed during their initial phone conversation. Once she arrives, she dowses to check on what she can't see—things happening at an energetic, nonvisual level. Depending on the client, she'll either dowse openly or discreetly, using a bracelet as a pendulum, for instance, or a body-dowsing method. At the front door, which she says is the most important place in the house, she'll ask, "Is there any sort of an underground issue with water or energies or geopathic stress that I need to be aware of, yes or no?" If there is a problem with a water vein flowing under the front door, she simply asks for it to be moved: "Would you be willing to move your path of water in order to make this a more healthful entrance for the family?" In the bedroom, placement of the bed in the "command position" is key in feng shui. But Weklar always dowses to make sure that what looks like the ideal location for the bed from a visual perspective actually is the best spot, and that there aren't any nonbeneficial energies at play. Sometimes a water vein under a bed *isn't* a problem. "For some people, they can handle being on top of water," Weklar said. "It's beneficial to them. I always check."

Bull agrees that not every stream or natural emanation can be harmful to the people living above it. "Every job is a custom job," he likes to say. Nature has a reason for that stream to be flowing that way. It's important to determine whether it is causing you any harm before you attempt to make some kind of change.

Dowsers who specialize in clearing energies in a home sometimes come across spirit entities or energetic imprints from people who lived there before. Bull has had success clearing entities remotely. One case involved a historic property that over the years had been a stagecoach station, a school, even a home for unwed mothers. A California development group bought the house and the surrounding acreage with the provision that they would restore the building. But Bull said the developers were particularly vexed by the way things were going.

"They had more accidents than any project they'd ever been on," he said. So they contacted Bull after the most recent accident, involving a carpenter working on a ladder. Apparently, the man peeked through a second-story window and saw an apparition that looked like a pirate. "And he was stunned and he fell off the ladder and hurt himself. So they were sick and tired of having people get hurt." As he often does, Bull enlisted the aid of his wife to remotely clear the place of entities. "And they never had another, not even a minute of time lost after that."

Sometimes, people call Weklar specifically to clear a home of the spirit of a deceased relative that is hanging around. Others don't know what's wrong; they jus sense the place feels *icky*. "If I get to a place and I feel the ick, but I know that they wouldn't be able to hear it, what I do is tell them I'm picking up a heaviness." Weklar then suggests a space clearing to get rid of the negative energy. "People get more hung up with the verbiage, I find, in my experience. If I said it just needs to have some fresh energy, it would be more accepted than saying, 'Wow, I think you've got an entity in this room.'"

There are different techniques for doing a space clearing and sending entities on their way. Bull likes to make a forceful request that the entity leave that home where they don't belong and cross over to the spirit world. Edith Greene tries a gentler approach. She likes to tell spirits that she can "help them cross over" to where they belong. She goes through a ritual with her rods, moving one from the floor to the top of the spirit's head, and tells it, "You reach up and take hold of your angels and they'll help you go." Weklar, after ʾowsing to determine what kind of an entity is present, ˙des on what kind of a cure to use. There are various ui ceremonies to clear a home, involving sound ˄ing or using bells), scent (burning incense), ˄t (tracing a pattern through a home while ˡly, the windows and doors are opened

THE HOME

before the ceremony, so that the old can go out and the new fresh energy can come in.

DOWSING YOUR HOME

To discover whether anything is harming you within your home, make a sketch of the floor plan of your house or apartment. Take a few deep breaths to center yourself and connect to source energy or universal consciousness. Ask, "Is there anything that is noxious or toxic to me or my family in this house?" If you get a yes, ask whether the energy is natural or man-made. If it is natural, hold your pencil over each room of the house with your pendulum in the other hand, and dowse to see where the problem is. Once you zero in on the room, determine whether the problem is caused by an underground water vein. If so, take your L-rods into the room and dowse where the water veins are running. If you find that a bed is on top of the water vein, ask whether it is adversely affecting you. If it is, see if you can position the bed to avoid the area. But if you can't, set your intention to change the situation. Working with the powers of nature, ask whether the energy can be transformed into something beneficial. If it can, set your intention to transmute the energy in that way. Check again by dowsing. If the energy is still there, ask whether the water vein can go around your home without causing any disruption to anyone or anything else. If so, set your intention to bring that about.

EASY STEPS TO CHECK THE ENERGY
IN YOUR HOME

- Center yourself and connect to universal energy.
- Ask whether there is any energy that is nonbeneficial to you or your family in your home.
- Ask whether the problem is natural or man-made.
- Zero in on the location of the problem, either by walking through your home or by using your pendulum on a sketch of your floor plan.
- Reposition pieces of furniture (primarily beds) if you find they are over a problem water vein or near electromagnetic fields from appliances.
- If you can't solve the problem that way, ask whether the energy can be transformed into something beneficial.

If you find that the problem in your home is man-made—for example, caused by the electromagnetic fields given off by appliances and electrical wiring—dowse your sketch to find the areas that are problematic in your home. Then see if you can determine whether the issue is something you can act on, like moving a television set to a better location. If you want to double-check your results, there are electromagnetic frequency sensors, called EMF detectors, that you can buy that will show where unsafe levels of EMFs are being given off by electrical outlets, appliances, and wiring in your home.

~ 13 ~

Advanced Techniques

In a classroom in Washington, DC, on a rainy weeknight in spring, a handful of middle-aged students stared intently at a rectangle on a piece of paper in front of them. Slowly and carefully, they dangled a pendulum over every inch of their makeshift map and asked themselves the question, "Where is the quarter?" On a table at the end of the room, a thick placemat covered the coin hidden under the lower left-hand corner. The students had no idea where the quarter was, but when they dowsed on their maps, more than half of them hit the spot exactly. Amazed by their own success, the students had boosted their dowsing skills from novice to advanced in less than two hours.

Many different dowsing specialties rely on the technique of map dowsing. It can be invaluable when dowsing for water on a large piece of land, or in finding lost people or animals. Any dowsing that is done remotely and requires locating something can use this method.

If you were to go outside with a pair of L-rods and try to find water, you could walk around asking yourself the question, "Where is the nearest source of water?" This is "shoe-leather dowsing." You are actually walking over the source, picking up on the vibration of what you are trying to find. It takes time to cover a large area and you need to be on location to do it.

But most professionals start out with maps. It's much faster and more convenient. It enables them to work on properties hundreds and in some cases thousands of miles from their homes. Leroy Bull once sited several wells for a residential development on a mountaintop in Costa Rica. First, the developers e-mailed the maps and Bull narrowed down some target areas, drawing a box around them. He enlarged them on a photocopier and dowsed again. Had the project been a local one, he would have gone to the property at that time to pinpoint exactly where to site the well. But since he was thousands of miles away, he did the next best thing. The developer took digital photographs of the areas Bull had targeted and sent them to him. In the first, "there happened to be a great big dandelion right in the middle of the box that they had photographed. That's where the well was going to be. And so I sent them back an e-mail that said, 'Drill right down through that dandelion. You're going to get about seventy-five gallons a minute.'" He was wrong. They got about ninety gallons per minute, nearly three times more than any well pumping in that area of Costa Rica.

Map dowsing is a more nuanced skill than simply picking up on the energy of something in front of you. It requires some practice. But it can be invaluable in tracking down something or someone in a very large area—in essence, finding the needle in the haystack.

Harold McCoy, a master dowser in Arkansas, once tracked down a stolen harp for a well-known psychoanalyst and academic in Berkeley, Dr. Elizabeth Lloyd Mayer. The incident so startled and intrigued her that she wrote a book about the experience and other psi events called *Extraordinary Knowing: Science, Skepticism, and the Inexplicable Powers of the Human Mind*. In it, she describes her first interaction with McCoy:

Harold picked up the phone—friendly, cheerful, heavy Arkansas accent. I told him I'd heard he could dowse for lost objects and that I'd had a valuable harp stolen in Oakland, California. Could he help locate it?

"Give me a second," he said. "I'll tell you if it's still in Oakland." He paused, then: "Well, it's still there. Send me a street map of Oakland and I'll locate that harp for you." Skeptical—but what, after all, did I have to lose?—I promptly overnighted him a map. Two days later, he called back. "Well, I got that harp located," he said. "It's in the second house on the right on D___ Street, just off L___ Avenue."

Sure enough, that's exactly where the harp was. Mayer drove to Oakland, found the house, wrote down the address, and called the police. The "tip" wasn't enough to justify a search warrant, so Mayer posted signs in the neighborhood offering a reward for a lost harp. A few days later, a man called and told her he knew where the harp was and arranged to return it in exchange for the reward.[1]

Moving targets can be trickier, of course. But they are not impossible, says Leroy Bull. "Once you are entrained on a target, then what the target is doesn't matter very much. But there are some variables in pets and the first one is, are they tethered or caged somewhere so you can actually tag them on the nose if you are map dowsing, or are they running? And the running ones are kind of hard." In that case, Bull attempts to dowse into the future with questions like, "Where will the dog be on Saturday?"

Bruce Irwin, who prefers not to dowse questions in the future, does it a different way. He asks, "In which direction is this dog headed?" Then he sends the owner with some of her dirty laundry to an intersecting path along the way, hoping the dog, with its superior powers of scent, will hang around long enough for the owner to retrieve him.

Irwin has a library of atlases, one for every state in the union. Filled with topographical maps, they offer a bird's-eye view of the land, as if you were flying overhead. Occasionally, though, he's had to rely on a hand-drawn map. Several years ago, he got an urgent call from a woman in Miami who had lost her pet cockatiel, Tutu. The only information she could give him was that the bird flew out an open screen porch door that morning. With time of the essence, and with the woman unable to identify her location on a map, Irwin took a blank piece of paper and placed a dot at the center to represent the back porch of the home. That was the search center, from which he then dowsed how far and in which direction the bird flew. Irwin determined that Tutu was on a stationary perch, twenty feet off the ground. He told the woman to head five hundred yards south by southeast and look up. That's exactly where she found her bird, sitting on the branch of a tree.[2]

Bull has written a workbook, *The Art and Craft of Map Dowsing*, which includes more than a dozen techniques and exercises to practice map dowsing.[3] An easy one is the ruler method. Using your pendulum, go across the top of your map asking your question. For instance, "Where is my dog, Spot?" When you get a positive swing, make a small pencil mark at the edge of the page. Then go down the vertical edge of the map. Again, when you get a positive swing, make a mark. You now have two marks in the margins of your map, one at the top and one on the side. Using your ruler as a guide, follow the lines across and down to find the intersecting point.

Another map-dowsing technique is the block method. Divide your map in quarters and number them one through four. Then ask, "Where is my dog, Spot?" When you get a positive spin on a section, mark that block into four smaller quarters. Basically, you work in smaller and smaller blocks until you pinpoint the location.

If you want, you can photocopy the section of the map so you can mark directly on it. You can also enlarge a section to get a more detailed reading. Another idea is to make a clear overlay with a grid pattern in permanent marker: A, B, C, and D across the top, and 1, 2, 3, 4 down the side. Then you can use this grid over any map you need to dowse.

Of course, anything can be a map. An outline of the human body can be a map you can dowse to pinpoint an area of concern relating to your health. A sketch of your house plan can be a map to dowse when you lose something. Make a simple hand-drawn map of your yard and see if you can find any coins that have been dropped, or something of value that has been buried on your property.

Once you accept the quantum physics principle that the parameters of time and space do not apply to the nonlocal mind, map dowsing does not seem like an impossible feat. But it is an advanced skill that takes some practice. Don't be discouraged if you can't do it immediately. Like all dowsing skills, it can be enhanced over time just by doing more of it. The next time you forget where you placed your car keys, pick up your pendulum, sketch out your floor plan, and try map dowsing to find them.

THE POWER OF INTENTION

Much has been written about the power of intention, and the ability of our thoughts to create our reality. But it takes a certain kind of thought, an extremely focused thought, to bring about the changes we want to see. Most people give up or become bored before they ever see a result. That may be because our have-it-now society places such emphasis on instant gratification. Attention wanes. It's hard to keep our minds focused on a clear intention when the demands of modern life keep us running 24-7. Most people spend nearly all their time with their consciousness centered on day-to-day concerns and material needs. Our consciousness is flabby. It's not getting the kind of workout it needs to become a powerful co-creator in this quantum world we live in. Dowsers, on the other hand, know how to make some surprising things happen simply with the power of the mind.

The kinds of changes Leroy Bull can make on behalf of his clients seem impossible. He can crush a water vein, or divert it from coming into a house. How? By actively focusing his intention. As impossible as that might seem, Bull is not alone in saying he has this ability. Many water dowsers say they move secondary water veins into a main vein in order to replenish an existing well that is going dry.

Bruce Irwin explained that a combination of factors is necessary to successfully divert a vein: intention, focus, a genuine need, and a good aerial map. "Locally, I move veins with a rebar driven into the ground with a sledgehammer and then I smack the piece of rebar sticking out of the ground in the direction that I want the water to move," he said. "But you can do that also remotely with a pencil on a piece of paper by tapping the end of the pencil. So, it's pretty unbelievable stuff."

There are limitations, though. The feeder veins can't be deeper than the existing well, for instance. Otherwise, you'd have to defy gravity and move the water upward. Also, there's a limit to how far you can move a vein. "It is very difficult to permanently divert a vein for an additional supply more than 30 degrees off of its present course. If you try to bend that more than 30 degrees, you're gonna end up babysitting it every couple of weeks because it will go back in memory to its old route," Irwin said. He currently is working on a remote project to replenish a well in New Zealand.

Bull explains it this way: "The truth is it all boils down to frequency. Frequency is how your mind works on everything, on anything. Once you learn that you are connected and *become* connected to the frequencies, virtually anything can be done."

When Bull first started working remotely on moving water veins, he would map-dowse a property and find all the smaller water veins that were causing the problem. Then he would stick a pin in them. "I would literally take a straight pin and a map of their house and ... stick that pin in the map where I wanted that to change." The pin took the place of the rebar in the ground, and instead of pounding it with a sledgehammer, all it took was focused intention and some taps in the right direction with a pencil. But even that proved unnecessary to Bull. Several years back, he got a call from someone in Maryland with a wet basement. "In that case, I didn't put any pins through any paper. My wife and I just sat down in our meditative states," he said.

Bull still dowsed where the problem veins were, but he didn't need the symbolic action with the pins. He only needed his thoughts. When he was done, he told his clients, "Give it about two weeks to make sure. And then any time the basement gets wet after that, call me. Well, ten months later, he called me and it still wasn't wet. And they were back in their wet season. So it worked. It is *evidentially* true. That's all. You just intend that any little water veins that are bumping along in the shallower or shallow depths, or that are bumping into the basement wall, go some other place that is harmful to none in the universe."

Working on a map with a pencil, Louis Matacia follows a similar procedure. He asks himself, "Where can we divert this water into that well?" He explained, "And then I go down the stream and bingo, the pendulum will tell me where. And so I take a pencil and I put it on the stream, and I tap the pencil toward that well, and the water goes into that well and resupplies it with another vein, and they don't have to drill a new well. That's so far out you can't talk to many people about it because they don't understand it. Now I don't personally understand it either, but I do it all the time. And so do all of the rest of the people around me. But it's unreal."

There is some scientific explanation for why mind-matter interactions are possible. Dean Radin, who conducts experiments in psi at the Institute of Noetic Sciences (IONS), explained the phenomenon of psycho-kinetic effects in *Entangled Minds*: "Anything that resides, even momentarily, in a quantum indeterminate state may be susceptible to influence from nonlocal minds. This predicts that the more inherent indeterminacy there is within an object, the more likely it can be influenced via thought (PK). Thus, it should be more difficult to mentally affect a rock than a bacterium."[4]

Water veins shift all the time with movement and vibration underground. It's not unheard of for a drilling rig to cause a vein to shift due to excessive vibrations of the machinery. Using a rebar and sledgehammer to move a vein seems entirely plausible when you understand that. But a pin and a pencil, or just intention alone? Many people are skeptical that thoughts can cause these kinds of changes in matter. Those who are open to dowsing and to other psi events don't feel the conflict in understanding the workings of the natural world.

The homeowner got the desired results and that was all that mattered to him. This goes to the heart of why so many people believe that dowsing works, and an equal number think it is New Age nonsense. It all depends on how open your mind is to seeing what's there. Science relies on evidence. But what if the evidence conflicts with the linear world of classical Newtonian physics? Stories like this, and so many other psi events, can be easily dismissed.

Consider the case of Edith Greene, who dowsed the municipal water supply for the town of Montgomery, Vermont. She is famous throughout the area for her dowsing ability and has a reputation for being able to remove radon from homes. When she helped site Montgomery's new wells, she was nearly hailed as a town hero. But a few months later, when the water tested positive for uranium, the situation looked grim. At a select-board meeting in front of the whole town, the news broke and the atmosphere in the room was tense. Then Greene called out, "I can move it." People nearly guffawed. But given the desperation of the situation, the town's attorney told her to go ahead and try. What had they to lose?

Greene walked those fields again, identifying every spot of uranium that was affecting the well, and moved them to a safe location with her intention. Her technique is to hold one L-rod on the spot and keep her eyes fixed on where she wants the uranium to go. Then she taps the rod firmly and commands, "Move that uranium over there." She dowses for the right spot to move it and if she has trouble deciding, "I ask my boss up above."

When the town's water was tested a few months later, the uranium was nearly gone, from seventy-six parts per billion down to an acceptable level of six. But that didn't satisfy Greene. When she heard that, she got to work again to find the remaining spots. The final testing found the water to be virtually uranium-free at 2.7 parts per billion.

Greene got results, but state officials and the town's selectmen could not believe that she had moved the uranium with intention. There had to be some other explanation—that the original testing was incorrect, or that the driller had contaminated the well by accident. When word leaked out that Greene had removed the uranium, the selectmen were in an awkward position. While they originally paid four hundred dollars for her dowsing services, they declined paying her second bill for working on the uranium. To do so would make these conservative, churchgoing town elders appear foolish, or worse. It simply could not fit within their worldview.[5]

Elizabeth Lloyd Mayer explained this phenomenon in her book *Extraordinary Knowing*. You can't see something if your mind isn't open to it. It's the same reason, she maintains, that so much good scientific evidence on psychic events is ignored. People will only believe what they think is possible.[6]

Louis Matacia agrees. "We don't go around telling too many people because they wouldn't comprehend how we do it. They don't believe it even though they see it. Even if you do it and repeat it, they still have trouble understanding how you did it."

To try an experiment with intention, get two identical water bottles. Put a piece of tape on the bottom of each and label one A and the other B. Now, pick up one bottle, note whether it is A or B, and cradle it in your hands. Close your eyes and send love to that bottle of water. *Intend* to give it your loving energy, as if it is a gift you are creating for someone. Now, put the bottles together and mix them up so that you don't know which is which. Take out your pendulum or dowsing tool and determine which one has the stronger, more positive energy. Chances are, you will pick the bottle you held with love. When I do this exercise in my classes, nearly every person picks the right bottle.

In *The Hidden Messages in Water*, Japanese research-er Masaru Emoto showed how water infused with the energy of love forms beautiful patterns when frozen, while negatively charged water forms crystals that are misshapen. He perfected an elaborate technique that allowed him to freeze individual water crystals and study them under the microscope to demonstrate the power of intention.[7] But you can test the energy of water, or any other substance you want, simply by using your pendulum and asking the right questions. You just proved that to yourself in this exercise, as well as proving that your *intention* created *change*. You affected the water in the bottle in a positive way, simply with your thoughts. Think about the implications for that in all other areas of your life. Continue working with intention, sharpening and focusing your thoughts, and eventually you may be able to divert a water vein, too.

Now that you are a dowser, you have opened your mind to an entirely new world of possibilities. You have repatterned your brain waves to activate the dowsing response. Your brain is not flabby. You have been actively exercising it, stepping into and out of higher states of consciousness with ease. Dowsing is a continuum, beginning when you first get a swing out of a pendulum or movement out of a pair of L-rods. You will gain more skill and accuracy the more you practice and trust in your intuitive abilities. Hold yourself and your intuitive skills in a place of scrupulous integrity, be of service in some way, and be grateful for your gift. Your intuitive mind is your birthright, and dowsing has provided a way to access it. As time goes on, you may find that you do not even need your dowsing tools. You ask a question and you know the answer without even picking up a pendulum. That stage is farther along the dowsing continuum. What Leroy Bull, Bruce Irwin, Louis Matacia, and Edith Greene can do simply with their focused intention is a highly advanced ability. But the most important requirement for getting to that level is to believe that it is possible.

~ 14 ~

Troubleshooting

Once you've been dowsing for a while, you will inevitably fall into a period when your accuracy seems off. You may get false readings, or you may have trouble connecting at all. Sometimes, people find that their pendulums are swinging the opposite way from what they're used to. When that happens, it becomes difficult to trust your intuition. How can you, when you don't know what you are doing wrong?

Here are some ideas to try if you find that you are having difficulty. First of all, make sure you are well rested. If you try to dowse too late at night, or when you are tired, you can get inconsistent answers. Get a good night's sleep and try again in the morning. You may find that eliminates the problem right there.

It's also a good idea to check whether your energy system is balanced. Sometimes, a particularly stressful day or an upsetting event can affect us to the point that our polarity becomes flipped. So your pendulum swinging yes can really mean that it is a no. A quick way to set things right is to do "the three thumps." Place your fingers on your collarbone and then drop them about an inch below and slightly toward the center. These are the K-27 points on the acupuncture meridian system. If the spots feel a little sore, you are in the right place. Tap the points firmly while taking deep breaths for about twenty seconds or so. Then drop your fingers down to your sternum, a few inches below the center, and tap on your thymus gland for about fifteen seconds. These techniques can help revitalize your energy system and bring it back into balance. In less than a minute, your dowsing can be back on track. To learn more about energy balancing, refer to Donna Eden's landmark book on the subject, *Energy Medicine*.[1]

Another suggestion is to go outside in nature and take some good, deep breaths. Take a walk, feeling as if you are pulling in energy from Mother Earth. John Wayne Blassingame, the master dowser in Vermont, likes to lean up against a big tree when he feels the need to ground himself before dowsing. Try it yourself. It is an amazingly simple and powerful way to recharge yourself.

Walking the path of a labyrinth can do the same thing. Labyrinths have been used since ancient times as a walking meditation and spiritual tool. You can sometimes find labyrinths on the grounds of churches and public parks. Go to www.labyrinthlocator.com to learn whether there's one near you.

Take time to meditate each day, preferably before you start an intuitive session. You can sit in your favorite spot with your hands palm-up in your lap, or in any position that feels comfortable to you. Close your eyes and take a few deep breaths. Start to concentrate on your higher self, the part of you that is divine and connects to the divine. Some people imagine the higher self residing at the top of the head, pulsing in their hands, or enveloping them as an aura. Ask your higher self to be with you and to connect to universal energy, the wisdom that is available to all of us.

Imagine pure golden light coming down from the universe and pouring into the top of your head. Feel the energy as it enters your body. Imagine the light filling you inside, starting at the top of your head, coming down into your shoulders, and deeper down into your heart. Imagine that healing light is moving throughout your body, going everywhere that you need it most.

Take a deep breath and, as you exhale, let go of any negative feelings you are aware of. Breathe in the light, knowing that you are connected to the source of universal wisdom.

Another meditation that is good to try before dowsing is one you do on your feet. Stand with your feet planted firmly about shoulder-width apart. Bring your attention to your feet and imagine that they have roots that go deep into the earth. Think about all the energy that is at the earth's core. Now imagine that swirling energy coming up from the earth into your feet. Continue bringing that energy up through your legs, up your spine, down your arms, all the way through your body. Now send that energy out through the top of your head, like a column of light going up into the heavens. You are connecting your energy with the sea of universal energy that we all have access to. Now reverse the process. Imagine the energy swirling overhead, and bring some of that energy down the column of light into the top of your head, down your spine, all the way through you until it reaches your toes. You can repeat the process several times until you feel grounded and energized.

If you'd rather not do a visualization, just use your breath as an anchor, concentrating on breathing in deeply, and then breathing out. You can place one hand on the top of your head and the other over your belly button. Bring your attention to the top of your head when you inhale, and move it to your navel when you exhale.

Many dowsers try to cultivate an "attitude of gratitude." Get in the habit of being thankful for your intuitive gift. Give silent thanks when you finish an intuitive session. Before you go to bed at night, spend a few moments contemplating everything that you are thankful for in your life. This simple step can make a world of difference in your emotional well-being and in your dowsing.

Remember to ask permission. Sometimes, we are in such a rush to get guidance on a topic that we skip the step of asking for permission. You can go through the steps of asking "May I, Can I, Should I." Or you can ask, "Do I have permission to dowse about this, am I capable of dowsing about this, and is this an appropriate time?" Make sure you are not asking the questions in a rote way. If you rush through them, you are basically assuming that you have permission even before you ask. Try to hold yourself in a meditative "beginner's mind," as you always should when tapping your intuition. Don't presume you know the answer before you start.

You might want to say a prayer or set an intention that your dowsing can be of service, especially if you are asking questions for someone else. Ask your ego to step aside and think of yourself as a channel for the information. Also, try not to think of yourself as special, at least where your dowsing ability is concerned. Once your ego gets attached to the idea that you have some kind of special gift, you just might find your accuracy failing.

Since part of dowsing is picking up electromagnetic fields, make sure you are working in an area that is free from disturbances. Don't dowse in front of the computer or the television if they are on. If you know that there is a section of your home that has beneficial energies for you, make a practice of dowsing there on a regular basis. Edith Greene likes to stand on a ley line she has determined runs right through her home. She plants her heels on the line whenever she needs a boost.

Even if you don't have your own personal ley line, you might have an area of your home that is special to you that would work just as well. Perhaps it is where you do your meditation, or sip your coffee in the morning. Perhaps you have a home altar, or a simple grouping of stones or some treasured pictures with a candle. Whatever location makes you feel at your energetic best is the right place to dowse, especially when you feel your dowsing may be off.

If you use a crystal or stone pendulum, it's a good idea to cleanse it from time to time, since crystals and stones can hold energetic vibrations. You can try running them under water, leaving them out in the sun, or, if they are not too delicate, placing them in a bowl of salt. If you don't have time for a full cleansing, try "pulling off" the old energy. Close your hand around the pendulum and then sweep it down and away from you, as if you were following a string trailing off from the tip. If you haven't cleaned your pendulum in a while and your dowsing seems off, try one of these cleansing techniques.

If you are still having trouble, check in with your subconscious about the reason. Ask if it is because of any negative beliefs or assumptions you may have about dowsing or accessing your intuition. If you get a yes, you can try to figure out exactly what is holding you back on a subconscious level, or you can go straight to the subconscious clearing we did at the beginning of chapter three. You may find it helpful to write down the different topics you are asking about. Then use your pendulum while dowsing over the page. Sometimes, it is easier to do a session this way, rather than hold all the questions in your head.

Whatever you do, keep practicing. That's the best way to get back on track with your dowsing. Take a pack of playing cards, turn a few cards face down, and dowse whether they are red or black. Start with three and work your way up to five or seven. That is how Bill Northern practiced until he built up the confidence to dowse professionally.

Or, if you'd like a more real-world way to test yourself, try picking up your pendulum when the phone rings. Ask yourself, "Is this someone I know?" Or "Is this someone in my family?" It's an easy way to get instant feedback about the accuracy of your dowsing.

Another way to verify whether you are getting correct information is to try some blind questions. Be sure to add a few that you know the answers to, like "My name is…" and "I live at…" If you get a negative response to those questions, you will confirm that your dowsing is still off.

TROUBLESHOOTING CHECKLIST

❑ Be well rested.

❑ Do an energy check.

❑ Go outside in nature.

❑ Ground yourself.

❑ Walk a labyrinth.

❑ Meditate.

❑ Remember to ask permission.

❑ Be grateful.

- ❏ Hold an intention to be of service.
- ❏ Ask your ego to step aside.
- ❏ Avoid dowsing around computers, televisions, and appliances.
- ❏ Dowse in your sacred space.
- ❏ Cleanse your pendulum.
- ❏ Do another clearing.
- ❏ Write down your questions.
- ❏ Practice with cards.
- ❏ Test yourself when the phone rings.
- ❏ Dowse blind.

 Conclusion

L earning to dowse is like building a bridge to the intuitive mind. Western society doesn't teach us to use that part of our brain. There is no primer for learning about intuition in school and there is no roadmap for trying to learn on our own. As a result, there is much human potential in our society that is going untapped.

Dowsing provides a bridge to inner wisdom, making it easier to cross the murky waters of the subconscious to gain the clear insight of our intuition. I wanted to write *Intuition in an Instant* to introduce this technique to people who hadn't heard about it before. I wanted to share how practical dowsing is, and show how it can be a tool to access our intuitive abilities. I hope you find, like most dowsers, that it changes your life for the better. It certainly allows you to experience more of the world around you than you ever would with just your five senses. Dowsing, in a sense, opens the shutters on a different world, a quantum world of energy and interconnectedness.

I am grateful to be able to share the stories of these amazing dowsers with you. What they can do is truly mind-boggling. But they all started out as beginner dowsers, like you. They are just a little farther along the intuitive path. Intuition is our birthright and dowsing is one way—a simple and practical way—that we can claim it.

If you've worked through the material in this book, I can guarantee that dowsing has already changed your life and expanded your view of what you think is possible. Just watching a pendulum swing, *directed by thought alone,* is enough to cause the initial shift. Practicing dowsing teaches you to activate the deepest brain wave states of theta and delta, which many people rarely access except during sleep. When you learn to dowse, you practice working with higher states of consciousness, and it literally changes your brain. New research into neuroplasticity shows that our brains have the ability to adapt, even at an advanced age. Dowsing allows us access to the insights of our deep subconscious and our intuitive radar even during normal waking consciousness.

I believe in the coming years we will see breakthroughs in scientific research on consciousness. Eventually, there will be a definitive explanation for how dowsing works.

Until then, keep practicing and decide whether *you* believe it works. It does for me. I have gotten correct answers to questions I could not possibly have known in any other way. I have helped friends make decisions by dowsing for them, and I pick up my pendulum to help me make decisions nearly every day. Dowsing is like checking in with my most basic intuition. I rely on it so much now, I wouldn't think of making a major choice without it. But of course, I have been wrong many times as well, especially when checking in about a subject where I have an emotional attachment. To me, that doesn't matter. Dowsing has given me a reliable technique to access my intuition and to train my brain in higher states of consciousness, something I could not master through traditional meditation. Dowsing *has* changed my life for the better. I hope you find it does the same for you.

Acknowledgments

This book has been a journey of sorts, and I want to thank all those people who supported me on the path. For listening without judgment, and for believing in me whether or not they believed in the phenomenon of dowsing, I'd like to thank my family: Jack Higham, Grace Klvana, Grace and Tom Trimmer, Liz and Bob Salerni, and Lenore and Jeff Fischman; and my friends: Jane Beard, Laura Hagmann, Holly Elwood, Meredith Self, Brigid Schulte, Meg Kimmel, April Witt, Donna St. George, Chris Chirico, Laura DeBruce, Tom Smith, Stacey Saltzman, Natalie Cary, Jessica Doran, Kristie Galic, Pam Thomas, Beth Gambitsky, Cathy Raines, Allyn Taylor, Laura Jappe, Anne Bartlett, Lisa Wenrich,

Sharon Roth, Daniel Thompson, Naomi Jacobson, and Kim Schraf.

For the opportunity to teach dowsing and further my understanding of the process, I am grateful to Debra Leopold of First Class, Inc., the Jung Society of Washington's Wisewoman Forum, and Six Sensory DC.

Every dowser I have met has taught me something valuable and helped me to refine my thinking about the craft. I am indebted to the master dowsers I interviewed for this book, and to the American Society of Dowsers for the community it provides and its commitment to sharing information.

Finally, I am grateful to Carrie Obry of Llewellyn Worldwide Ltd. and Lisa Hagan of the Paraview Literary Agency for seeing a place for this book in the publishing world.

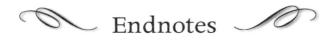 Endnotes

CHAPTER 1: BASICS OF DOWSING

1. T. Edward Ross and Richard D. Wright, *The Divining Mind* (Rochester, VT: Destiny Books, 1990), 49–53.

2. Christopher Bird, *The Divining Hand* (Atglen, PA: Whitford Press, 1993), 68.

3. Greg Nielsen and Joseph Polansky, *Pendulum Power* (Rochester, VT: Destiny Books, 1977), 23.

4. Bird, *The Divining Hand*, 72–92.

5. Online survey of American Society of Dowsers members, http://www.dowsers.org, completed March 2010.

CHAPTER 2: HOW IT WORKS:
THE SCIENCE BEHIND DOWSING

1. Edith Jurka, "Brain Patterns Characteristic of Dowsers," *The American Dowser* (Fall 1991): 8–14.

2. Anna Wise, *Awakening the Mind: A Guide to Mastering the Power of Your Brain Waves* (New York: Jeremy P. Tarcher/Penguin, 2002).

3. Letter from Albert Einstein to Herman Peisach of South Norwalk, CT (February 15, 1946): http://dowsingworks.com/einstein.html.

4. Dean Radin, *Entangled Minds* (New York: Paraview/Pocket Books, 2006), 8.

5. Russell Targ and Jane Katra, *Miracles of Mind* (Novato, CA: New World Library, 1998), 27.

6. Hans-Dieter Betz, "Unconventional Water Detection: Field Test of the Dowsing Technique in Dry Zones," *Journal of Scientific Exploration* (Vol. 9:1, article 1).

7. "One Million Dollar Paranormal Challenge," James Randi Educational Foundation, http://www.randi.org/site/index.php/1m-challenge.html.

CHAPTER 3: GETTING STARTED

1. This is a variation of a clearing taught to me by Jean Slatter, a writer and teacher on body-mind-spirit topics. http://www.creativemystic.com.

2. Walt Woods, *Companion to Letter to Robin,* fifth rev. http://www.lettertorobin.org.

CHAPTER 4: KICK-START YOUR INTUITION

1. I learned the technique of holding an intention to "raise the frequency" or energy of a situation from Raymon Grace, a master dowser based in Virginia. http://www.RaymonGrace.us.

CHAPTER 5: GETTING TO KNOW YOUR SUBCONSCIOUS

1. Enid Hoffman, *Huna: A Beginner's Guide* (Atglen, PA: Whitford Press, 1976), 43–44, 117–127.

2. Charlotte Berney, *Fundamentals of Hawaiian Mysticism* (Berkeley, CA: Crossing Press, 2000), 90–118.

CHAPTER 6: DOWSING FOR HEALTH AND HEALING

1. Meredith Self, an intuitive counselor and teacher, taught me the process of putting ego aside and asking to be a clear channel to assist another person, especially when doing health readings. http://www.sparkintuition.com.

CHAPTER 7: THE ENERGY BODY: BALANCING THE CHAKRAS

1. Donna Eden with David Feinstein, *Energy Medicine* (New York: Jeremy P. Tarcher/Putnam, 1998), 133–171.

2. Kalashatra Govinda, *A Handbook of Chakra Healing* (Saybrook, CT: Konecky & Konecky, 2004), 19–37.

CHAPTER 8: EXPLORING RELATIONSHIPS WITH DOWSING

1. Greg Nielsen, *Beyond Pendulum Power: Entering the Energy World* (Reno, NV: Conscious Books, 1988), 63–72.

2. Tsultrim Allione, *Feeding Your Demons: Ancient Wisdom for Resolving Inner Conflict* (New York: Little, Brown and Company, 2008), 55–73.

CHAPTER 10: INSTANT INTUITION FOR YOUR CAREER

1. Douglas Dean and John Mihalsky spent ten years studying intuition and business success at the New Jersey Institute of Technology. Their study was the basis for their book, *Executive ESP* (Upper Saddle River, NJ: Prentice Hall, 1974).

CHAPTER 11: FINDING WATER AND MORE

1. Greg Storozuk, "Dowsing: Simple Connections," *The American Dowser* (Fall/Winter 2009–10): 31–42.

2. Water for Life Decade Factsheet, http://www.un.org/waterforlifedecade/factsheet.html.

3. Bird, *The Divining Hand*, 199–214.

4. Louis J. Matacia, *Solutions through Dowsing: My Military Handbook* (Sterling, VA: L. J. Matacia, 2008).

CHAPTER 12: DOWSING IN THE HOME

1. Bachler's study was cited in an article by Simon Best, "What we don't know about earth radiation," in *The International Journal of Alternative and Complementary Medicine.*

CHAPTER 13: ADVANCED TECHNIQUES

1. Elizabeth Lloyd Mayer, *Extraordinary Knowing: Science, Skepticism, and the Inexplicable Powers of the Human Mind* (New York: Bantam Books, 2007), 2–3.

2. Bruce Irwin, "A Stationary Target," *The American Dowser* (Spring/Summer 2010), 32–33.

3. Leroy Keet Bull, *The Art and Craft of Map Dowsing: A Workbook* (Doylestown, PA: Minute Man Press, 2001), 2, 4.

4. Radin, *Entangled Minds*, 270.

5. Kate Daloz, "The Dowser Dilemma," *American Scholar* (Spring 2009), 87–99.

6. Mayer, *Extraordinary Knowing,* 143–147.

7. Masuru Emoto, *The Hidden Messages in Water* (Hillsboro, OR: Beyond Words Publishing, 2004).

CHAPTER 14: TROUBLESHOOTING

1. Eden, *Energy Medicine*, 63.

Bibliography

Allione, Tsultrim. *Feeding Your Demons: Ancient Wisdom for Resolving Inner Conflict*. New York: Little, Brown and Company, 2008.

Arntz, William, Betsy Chasse, and Mark Vicente. *What the Bleep Do We Know!?* Deerfield Beach, FL: Heath Communications, 2005.

Berney, Charlotte. *Fundamentals of Hawaiian Mysticism*. Berkley, CA: Crossing Press, 2000.

Betz, Hans-Dieter. "Unconventional Water Detection: Field Test of the Dowsing Technique in Dry Zones," *Journal of Scientific Exploration*, Vol. 9:1, article 1.

Bird, Christopher. *The Divining Hand*. Atglen, PA: Whitford Press, 1993.

Bull, Leroy Keet. *The Art and Craft of Map Dowsing: A Workbook*, rev. ed. Doylestown, PA: Minute Man Press, 2001, 2006.

Daloz, Kate. "The Dowser Dilemma." *American Scholar*, Spring 2009.

Eden, Donna, with David Feinstein. *Energy Medicine*. New York: Jeremy P. Tarcher/Putnam, 1998.

Emoto, Masuru. *The Hidden Messages in Water*. Hillsboro, OR: Beyond Words Publishing, 2004.

Gawain, Shakti. *Creative Visualization*. Novato, CA: New World Library, 1978.

Govinda, Kalashatra. *A Handbook of Chakra Healing*. Saybrook, CT: Konecky & Konecky, 2004.

Hoffman, Enid. *Huna: A Beginner's Guide*. Atglen, PA: Whitford Press, 1976.

Irwin, Bruce. "A Stationary Target." *The American Dowser*. Spring/Summer 2010.

Jurka, Edith. "Brain Patterns Characteristic of Dowsers." *The American Dowser*, Fall 1991.

MacManaway, Patrick. *Energy Dowsing for Everyone*. London, UK: Southwater/Anness Publishing, 2001.

Matacia, Louis J. *Solutions through Dowsing, My Military Handbook*. Sterling, VA: L. J. Matacia, 2008.

Mayer, Elizabeth Lloyd. *Extraordinary Knowing: Science, Skepticism, and the Inexplicable Powers of the Human Mind*. New York: Bantam Books, 2007.

McTaggart, Lynne. *The Field: The Quest for the Secret Force of the Universe*. New York: HarperCollins Publishers, 2008.

Nielsen, Greg. *Beyond Pendulum Power: Entering the Energy World*. Reno, NV: Conscious Books, 1988.

Nielsen, Greg, and Joseph Polansky. *Pendulum Power*. Rochester, VT: Destiny Books, 1977.

Olson, Dale W. *The Pendulum Charts: Knowing Your Intuitive Mind*. Eugene, OR: Crystalline Publications, 1989.

Percy, Nigel. *The Essence of Dowsing*. Victoria, BC: Trafford Publishing, 2002.

Radin, Dean. *Entangled Minds*. New York: Paraview, 2006.

Ross, T. Edward and Richard D. Wright. *The Divining Mind*. Rochester, VT: Destiny Books, 1990.

Sharpe, Dora. *Universal Allergy Healing: A Mother's Story*. Bloomington, IN: AuthorHouse, 2007.

Storozuk, Greg. "Dowsing: Simple Connections." *The American Dowser*, Fall/Winter 2009–10.

Targ, Russell, and Jane Katra. *Miracles of Mind: Exploring Nonlocal Consciousness and Spiritual Healing.* Novato, CA: New World Library, 1998.

Wise, Anna. *Awakening the Mind: A Guide to Mastering the Power of Your Brain Waves.* New York: Jeremy P. Tarcher/Penguin, 2002.

Woods, Walt. *Letter to Robin: A Mini-Course in Pendulum Dowsing.* Oroville, CA: The Print Shoppe, 1990.

―――. *Companion to Letter to Robin: Learning to Dowse – Student Guide and Teachers' Syllabus.* www.lettertorobin.org

TO WRITE TO THE AUTHOR

If you wish to contact the author or would like more information about this book, please write to the author in care of Llewellyn Worldwide and we will forward your request. Both the author and publisher appreciate hearing from you and learning of your enjoyment of this book and how it has helped you. Llewellyn Worldwide cannot guarantee that every letter written to the author can be answered, but all will be forwarded. Please write to:

Kathryn Klvana
℅ Llewellyn Worldwide
2143 Wooddale Drive
Woodbury, MN 55125-2989

Please enclose a self-addressed stamped envelope for reply, or $1.00 to cover costs. If outside the U.S.A., enclose an international postal reply coupon.

Many of Llewellyn's authors have websites with additional information and resources. For more information, please visit our website at http://www.llewellyn.com.

GET MORE AT **LLEWELLYN.COM**

Visit us online to browse hundreds of our books and decks, plus sign up to receive our e-newsletters and exclusive online offers.

- Free tarot readings • Spell-a-Day • Moon phases
- Recipes, spells, and tips • Blogs • Encyclopedia
- Author interviews, articles, and upcoming events

GET SOCIAL WITH **LLEWELLYN**

Find us on
 **Facebook**
www.Facebook.com/LlewellynBooks

Follow us on
twitter
www.Twitter.com/Llewellynbooks

GET BOOKS AT **LLEWELLYN**

LLEWELLYN ORDERING INFORMATION

Order online: Visit our website at www.llewellyn.com to select your books and place an order on our secure server.

Order by phone:
- Call toll free within the U.S. at 1-877-NEW-WRLD (1-877-639-9753)
- Call toll free within Canada at 1-866-NEW-WRLD (1-866-639-9753)
- We accept VISA, MasterCard, and American Express

Order by mail:
Send the full price of your order (MN residents add 6.875% sales tax) in U.S. funds, plus postage and handling to: Llewellyn Worldwide, 2143 Wooddale Drive Woodbury, MN 55125-2989

POSTAGE AND HANDLING:
STANDARD: (U.S. & Canada)
(Please allow 12 business days)
$25.00 and under, add $4.00.
$25.01 and over, FREE SHIPPING.

INTERNATIONAL ORDERS (airmail only):
$16.00 for one book, plus $3.00 for each additional book.

Visit us online for more shipping options. Prices subject to change.

FREE CATALOG!

To order, call
1-877-
NEW-WRLD
ext. 8236
or visit our
website

OVER 100,000 SOLD!
Practical Guide to
PSYCHIC POWERS
AWAKEN YOUR SIXTH SENSE
Denning & Phillips

Practical Guide to Psychic Powers
DENNING & PHILLIPS

Because you are missing out on so much without them! Who has not dreamed of possessing powers to move objects without physically touching them, to see at a distance or into the future, to know another's thoughts, to read the past of an object or person, or to find water or mineral wealth by dowsing?

This book is a complete course—teaching you step-by-step how to develop the powers that actually have been yours since birth. Psychic powers are a natural part of your mind; by expanding your mind in this way, you will gain health and vitality, emotional strength, greater success in your daily pursuits, and a new understanding of your inner self.

You'll learn to play with these new skills, working with groups of friends to accomplish things you never would have believed possible. The text shows you how to make the equipment, do the exercises—many of them at any time, anywhere—and how to use your abilities to change your life and the lives of those close to you.

978-0-87542-191-9, 288 pp., $5\frac{3}{16}$ x 8   **$11.95**

Tea Leaf
Reading

For Beginners

Your Fortune in a Tea Cup

CAROLINE DOW

Tea Leaf Reading for Beginners

Your Fortune in a Teacup

CAROLINE DOW

More people than ever are discovering the restorative benefits of tea and the life-enriching divinatory practice of tea-leaf reading. In answer to the surging popularity of this healthful and mystical beverage, *Tea Leaf Reading for Beginners* teaches readers how to read and interpret tea-leaves in six simple steps.

This complete guidebook explores the origins of tea and tea-leaf reading, ways of giving readings, divination ethics, tea's medicinal uses, herbal infusion preparation, and how to host a tea party. For quick and easy interpretation, hundreds of symbols and their meanings are included, organized by theme—animals, sun signs, plants, shapes, and many others.

978-0-7387-2329-7, 312 pp., 5³⁄₁₆ x 8   **$15.95**

COSMIC

ANNE JIRSCH

"Jirsch has taken complicated and abstract ideas and turned them into user-friendly concepts and techniques. The results will be life changing!"
—Paul McKenna, best-selling author of *Change Your Life in 7 Days*

How to Harness

the Invisible Power

Around You to

Transform Your Life

ENERGY

Cosmic Energy

*How to Harness the Invisible Power Around You
to Transform Your Life*

ANNE JIRSCH

Some people seem to lead a charmed life—they get what they want, they're in the right place at the right time, and even when they experience setbacks, they land on their feet. They're not just lucky—they're attuned to their cosmic energy.

Renowned psychic Anne Jirsch teaches readers how to connect with the flow of the universe to dramatically improve their lives. Using current studies, client examples, and personal stories, she explains a variety of highly effective techniques, from visualization and manifesting to working with etheric energy and thought field therapy.

Once the reader understands the basics of cosmic energy, Jirsch reveals how they can use the knowledge to improve their relationships, health, career, and finances.

978-0-7387-2125-5, 264 pp., 6 x 9,   **$16.95**

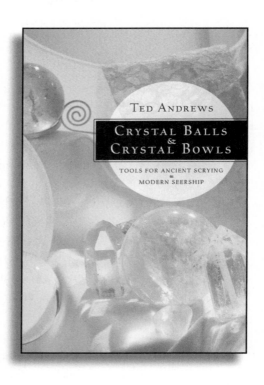

TED ANDREWS

CRYSTAL BALLS & CRYSTAL BOWLS

TOOLS FOR ANCIENT SCRYING & MODERN SEERSHIP

Crystal Balls & Crystal Bowls
Tools for Ancient Scrying & Modern Seership

TED ANDREWS

Quartz crystal balls and crystal bowls are popular magical tools. Yet, not everyone understands the extent of their power and multipurpose potential. Ted Andrews reveals how these dynamic instruments can be used for divination, astral projection, spirit communication, healing, and reaching higher states of consciousness.

Readers will learn many methods of crystal gazing, along with ways to enhance this practice with candles, fragrances, and elixirs. Also included are techniques for divining with water, communicating with angels and spirit guides, developing clairvoyance, and activating creativity. This updated edition also contains new illustrations.

978-1-56718-026-8, 256 pp., 6 x 9   **$15.95**

Scrying

For Beginners

Use Your Unconscious Mind to
See Beyond the Senses

DONALD TYSON

Scrying for Beginners

*Use Your Unconscious Mind to
See Beyond the Senses*

DONALD TYSON

Includes special offer for a free scrying sheet.

Scrying for Beginners is for anyone who longs to sit down before the mirror or crystal and lift the rolling grey clouds that obscure their depths. Scrying is a psychological technique to deliberately acquire information by extrasensory means through the unconscious mind. For the first time, all forms of scrying are treated in one easy-to-read, practical book. They include such familiar methods as crystal gazing, pendulums, black mirrors, Ouija™ boards, dowsing rods, aura reading, psychometry, automatic writing, and automatic speaking. Also treated are ancient techniques not widely known today, such as Babylonian oil scrying, fire gazing, Egyptian lamp scrying, water scrying, wind scrying, ink scrying, shell-hearing, and oracular dreaming.

978-1-56718-746-5, 320 pp., 5³⁄₁₆ x 8 $14.95

Divination

For Beginners

Reading the Past, Present & Future

SCOTT CUNNINGHAM

Divination for Beginners
Reading the Past, Present & Future
SCOTT CUNNINGHAM

There's no need to visit a soothsayer or call a psychic hotline to glimpse into your future or to uncover your past. You can become your own diviner of things unseen with the many methods outlined in this book, written by popular author Scott Cunningham.

Here you will find detailed descriptions of both common and unusual divinatory techniques, each grouped by the tools or techniques used to perform them. Many utilize natural forces such as water, clouds, smoke, and the movement of birds. Also discussed are the more advanced techniques of Tarot, Palmistry, and the I Ching.

978-0-7387-0384-8, 246 pp., 5³⁄₁₆ x 8 **$13.95**

To order, call 1-877-NEW-WRLD
Prices subject to change without notice
Order at Llewellyn.com 24 hours a day, 7 days a week!

Palm
Reading

For Beginners

Find Your Future in the Palm of Your Hand

Soloman
Ring

Girdle
of Venus

Self
Confidence

Fate Line

Heart Line

Life Line

RICHARD WEBSTER

Palm Reading for Beginners

Find Your Future in the Palm of Your Hand

RICHARD WEBSTER

Announce in any gathering that you read palms and you will be flocked by people thrilled to show you their hands. When you are have *finished Palm Reading for Beginners*, you will be able to look at anyone's palm (including your own) and confidently and effectively tell them about their personality, love life, hidden talents, career options, prosperity, and health.

Palmistry is possibly the oldest of the occult sciences, with basic principles that have not changed in 2,600 years. This step-by-step guide clearly explains the basics, as well as advanced research conducted in the past few years on such subjects as dermatoglyphics.

978-1-56718-791-5, 240 pp., 5³⁄₁₆ x 8 $13.95